We Always Wore Sailor Suits

SUSANNA AGNELLI

We Always Wore Sailor Suits

THE VIKING PRESS NEW YORK

First published in 1975 by The Viking Press, Inc.
625 Madison Avenue, New York, N.Y. 10022

Published simultaneously in Canada by
The Macmillan Company of Canada Limited

LIBRARY OF CONGRESS CATALOGING IN PUBLICATION DATA
Agnelli, Susanna, 1922–
We always wore sailor suits.
1. Agnelli, Susanna, 1922–   I. Title.
CT1138.A36A37   945.091′092′4 [B]   75-16338
ISBN 0-670-75322-x

Printed in U.S.A.

TO MY CHILDREN

"Maybe that's all understanding is—a terrific familiarity."

When a publisher friend of mine asked me to write this book, I did not know that he asks every woman he meets to write a book for him.

He really wanted it to be about fascism or the life of a rich family in Fascist Italy.

It happens that I was born in 1922, the same year in which Mussolini became Italy's dictator, and was married in 1945, the year in which fascism was finally and completely defeated, Mussolini died, and the war ended.

So the book turned out to be the story of myself during those Fascist years, and I am afraid my publisher was rather disappointed. He was expecting more scandal, more gossip, more names.

I wrote what I remembered; not what others told me I should remember. Sometimes I wrote episodes which, I discovered afterward, did not correspond to reality—for instance, that Axel Munthe had asked my grandmother Princess Jane to stop drinking. I left it as written because when I was a child that was what I believed.

I was told that I hardly mention the fact that my grandfather founded Fiat in 1899. In Italy books have been written about him and they are full of dates and facts. To me he was "Il Nonno" or "Il Senatore"; as Galeazzo Ciano was a friend, the Princess of Trabia was Raimondo's grandmother, and Malaparte was a man who loved my mother.

This is my life as I remember it until the day I got married.

Part One

The corridor was long, with rooms opening onto it from either side. Halfway down the corridor was the nursery. There were many of us and we had many governesses—they came from far away to Turin in Piedmont, the northern part of Italy which borders on France. In 1929 there were already five of us, Clara, the eldest, being nine years old. Miss Parker, mousy haired and plain, was the head governess, but other young girls came and went to teach us French or to look after the younger children and when another baby was born, a new nanny would appear. They sat in the nursery and complained about the cold, or the heating, or the maids, or the weather, or us. In winter the light bulbs were almost always burning. The Turin light that came in through the window was thick and gray. We always wore sailor suits: blue in winter, blue and white at mid-season, and white in the summer. For dinner, we changed into elegant frocks and short silk socks. My brother Gianni changed into another sailor suit.

Bathtime before dinner was noisy, full of splashes and jokes. We crowded into the bathroom and bathtub and the maids were driven mad. They brushed and combed our hair, which was very long and curly, and tied it with enormous black ribbons. Miss Parker would appear and when she had gathered us all she would say, "Let's go, and don't make a noise."

We rushed like crazy down the corridor, into the marble entrance, around the corner, hanging onto the marble pillar of the staircase, and into the little dining room, where we stood panting. "I told you not to rush," said Miss Parker. "One day you will hurt yourselves and you will only have yourselves to thank."

Our food was always what we disliked the most. I think it was part of our British education. We were made to eat everything that was put on our plates. Turnips and meat, where hard and elastic little nerves appeared, were my special nightmare. If you did not finish what was on your plate, it was brought back at the next meal.

The sweet we chose in turns, one day each. When it came to Maria Sole's turn we said, "Now, for God's sake, don't choose *crème caramel*, which we all hate." Invariably Miss Parker would ask, "Now, what sweet is it going to be tomorrow, Maria Sole? It's your turn." She would hesitate, blush, and murmur, *"Crème caramel."*

"But, why on earth do you go on saying *'crème caramel'*?" we tormented her as soon as Miss Parker had left the room. "I can't think of anything else to say."

And to this day I have not discovered if she really liked that damned *crème caramel* more than anything else, and did not dare admit it, or if the effort of thinking was too great.

After lunch we would go for long walks across the town and up the Piazza d'Armi, where the soldiers did their maneuvering. Only when it was raining were we allowed under the *portici* which follow the greater part of the center of Turin, and then we could look at the shop windows. We could look at them without stopping because "A walk is a walk and not dragging around, which gives you no exercise." Turin has always been known for its *pasticcerie*. In the windows were luscious cakes and cream-filled biscuits and chocolates and marzipan, shiny and lighted, and mountains of *brioches* and colored fondants on round plates like flowers, but never did we dream that one could enter the shop and buy those tempting delicacies. "Never eat between meals, it ruins your appetite" was an unbroken rule, one we never discussed.

So we walked for miles, sailor coats and round little sailor

hats with "H.M.S. Something or Other" written on the
band around the hat, Miss Parker in the middle and two of
us on one side and one or two of us on the other side until it
was time to go home. We looked enviously at the children
who were allowed to play on the Viali of the Corso Duca di
Genova or in the public gardens. There were clusters of *balie*
(wet nurses) in their colored skirts, lace aprons, and with
bright silk scarves on their heads held by pins of golden
filigree. They all wore identical black fur jackets which was
part of the trousseau which employers gave them when they
went to somebody's house to breast feed the baby of the
family. In the 1920s and 1930s the *balie* usually ended by
staying on many years as nannies. The babies sat in prams,
the older children played with one another. They had
hoops, or scooters, or marbles. They had friends, they
quarreled, they talked, they hopped, they shouted. We
walked. Miss Parker disapproved of the *balie* who would
pull down the drawers of the children and say "Pss, pss,
pss," holding them against a tree.

There were a few families who had English governesses,
but then Miss Parker would say it was not right that we
should play with children whose parents did not come to
the house. "Don't forget that you are an Agnelli," she
would add.

At four o'clock we came home, we did our homework, we
played. As I helped Gianni with his electric train and steam
locomotive, I dreaded the coming of dark and night. We
saw our parents after we had finished our dinner and they
were preparing for theirs. If they didn't have too many
guests, we would then sit in the library with them until they
went into the dining room. Occasionally we were allowed
around the table, but as we tended to play with the lighted
candles and make a nuisance of ourselves, we were soon
dismissed. We sat again in the nursery. Sometimes Miss

Parker would read aloud, or we would play a game until, "Time for bed now. Wash your teeth, and I'll come in and say good-night in ten minutes. Don't forget to fold your clothes and say your prayers."

I knelt in my bedroom and prayed desperately. I kissed the crucifix and the Madonna at the head of my bed and only asked not to be too terrified and to be able to go to sleep and not wake up in the middle of the night. I got into bed—we each had a room to ourselves—and when Miss Parker came in I threw my arms around her neck and hugged her and begged her to leave my door open just a little bit so that I could see some light. "No, no," she answered quietly, "you must learn to sleep in the dark. It is silly to be afraid."

When she left, for a short time I could see the light coming from the nursery through a crack at the bottom of my door, but when that went out, I was frozen by fear at the idea of being in the dark. I would get up and go to the bathroom. I would walk into my brother's and sisters' rooms and look at them sleeping, but it was as if they had not been there because I couldn't talk to them and they did not see me. It was as if I were dead. I got even more frightened. I went back to my bed and wet it to get a sensation of warmth and life. Sometimes I shouted out. Nobody heard me or wanted to hear me. When I woke up in the morning the only thing that mattered was that it was morning and people were around and alive. In the daytime I forgot.

The maid Vigiassa was a great source of amusement for us. She was generally despised in the house because her husband had left her with a small daughter and gone to America. She had red hair and was covered in freckles. She wanted to be called "*La balia* Vigia" even though she had not come to us as a wet nurse, but as a *balia asciutta*, or dry nurse, to Cristiana. Then she had become a maid to the

children and was forever getting into trouble with the
governesses and nannies. She respected only "La Miss
Pack" because she was just and fair, "even if she was a
Protestant." She was terrified of our father, so when he was
very good-humored we would convince him to summon
Vigiassa to his room before dinner as if he were going to
give her a scolding. She would appear, redder than ever,
covered in sweat, looking around with tormented, terrified
eyes until she saw us hiding somewhere in the room
laughing. My father would say, "It's all right, Vigia, I
wanted to know how you were." Afterward she would cry
and say to us, "Don't do this to me, I am afraid. I sweat and
then your mother says I smell. It is true. I smell because I
have red hair. I can't help it, even if I wash much more
than the others." We laughed. She sat at the little table in
the *guardaroba*, where they ironed my mother's clothes, and
ended up singing in a sad, monotonous wail, "He's gone to
'Merica. He's gone away."

*T*he part of the house that looked onto the Via
Papacino was ours, the children's. There was a covered
terrace which was later turned into a gymnasium. Our
parents' rooms looked onto the Corso, where the chestnut
trees bordered the alley in the middle of the street. On that
side were also the library and the sitting room and the
drawing room, which all opened onto the marble entrance
and stairway.

The third part of the house, where the pantries and the
kitchen and the servants' quarters and the linen room were,
looked onto the Via Avogadro. In this part of the house was

a small study, where we had private lessons. It was gay and full of books. Perhaps it was gay because it was in the servants' quarters, and there was work and laughter. The three parts of the house embraced the courtyard which had a round marble fountain in the middle. In the spring we bicycled around and around.

When we were ten years old we began the *ginnasio* and were in school; before that we were given lessons at home. Signorina Corsi was neurotic and complicated; certainly not the person Miss Parker would have chosen as a teacher for us. To begin with, she insisted on being served a cup of *cappuccino* at ten thirty and this was against all Miss Parker's principles. But, as Signorina Corsi told us almost every day, she had declared that she would not accept to teach us unless she was served her cup of *cappuccino*. If she did not have it she would faint, she had explained, and her terms had been reluctantly accepted. Now she had a right to her *cappuccino*, and a very bad one it was, she never missed telling us. The coffee was weak and lukewarm and the milk boiled with the skin in it, even though it was brought on a silver tray in a silver coffeepot by a liveried footman.

Signorina Corsi would throw both her hands toward the ceiling and wave them in the air like little flags to dry the sweat off. She was very sensitive, she said, and had to wear dress shields under her arms because of perspiration. She had big mauve circles under her eyes and a long, sad, pale face. You could smell her perspiring, and on the rare occasion when my father came into the room to inquire about our studies, she pulled her blouse away from her front so as to air her armpits. My father would leave immediately. He disliked Signorina Corsi and all her hysterical attitudes. "*Povera* Anna," Signorina Corsi would say, talking about herself. And she would, now and then, in a faraway tone, allude to a certain captain. One afternoon Vigiassa came into the nursery and murmured something about Signorina Corsi. Miss Parker said, "Tch, tch," as if to a bird making too much noise in a cage, and then moving her head from one side to another in a disapproving way she put on her coat and went out; an unheard of thing at this time of the day.

We gathered from the maids that Signorina Corsi had tried to commit suicide because of the captain. She did not come to give us lessons for a week, then appeared paler and with even deeper circles under her eyes, looking more than ever like a dead fish under a magnifying glass. Nobody ever mentioned a word about the episode.

Suicides were very fashionable at the time. The maids who fell in love with the butler (he was a great lady-killer) were forever taking sleeping pills in those rooms upstairs where they lived. "It's all your fault, Virginia," I once heard my grandmother say to my mother. "You give them all of that beautiful silk underwear of yours, what do you expect? They have to show it to somebody." These, of course, were my mother's maids, who were elegant and refined and who looked down their noses at the other maids who went to bed with the footmen and the chauffeurs. These had quarrels and said terrible things to one another, but they did not try to commit suicide. It was above their station.

At the top of the back stairs there were rooms which were rented to other people. In one of them lived "La Pignolo." She was the children's dressmaker. You climbed the back stairs and stood turning the hand-bell, like a bicycle's, nailed onto her wooden door. When she opened the door, you were repelled by the smell of the cooking on the stove underneath the window—then attracted by the ruffled children's dresses hanging all around the room. Around you were materials of every shade, silks and taffetas and Swiss embroidery and ribbons of all sizes. In the middle of all this stood La Pignolo, built like an acorn with two little legs coming out of the bottom. When she sat on her stool in front of the sewing machine she was exactly like a picture from the Happy Family cards that we played with downstairs before going to bed. La Pignolo sewed and sewed. Whatever she touched became beautiful so that you forgot the smell of cold leftover soup which filled the small attic.

Also, the *portineria*, or *conciergerie*, smelled of food. The smell wafted in through the small door that opened to admit cars from the Corso into the courtyard. My mother hated the smell of onion and garlic and wouldn't allow them in the kitchen. But Giuseppina had been her personal maid for years before she married the *portiere*, Guglielmo, so she went on cooking onions and garlic to her heart's content and, her black eyes sparkling like *"jais,"* stood up to my mother's scoldings, answering that you had to give a man the food he likes. When we were sure that Miss Parker would not find out, Giuseppina would let us taste her appetizing dishes, full of tomatoes and strange flavors. Guglielmo was tall, good-natured, dumb, and handsome in his livery, while Giuseppina was small and pretty and as bright as a Piedmontese *madamin* could be. She answered the telephone and knew everything that went on all over the house.

In the middle of June they took us to school, a few blocks from our house, to be examined with the other children and gain admission to the next grade. The smell of ink and pencils and children's hair mingled with the cool air of the wide corridor and classrooms. The other children, who had spent the year together in the same classroom, looked at me, the *privatista*, with a mixture of curiosity and compassion. Instead of a pinafore, I wore my sailor suit, and my hair was unusually long and curly. The teacher called me to the desk. I walked up the three wooden steps and stood in front of the blackboard. She questioned me on geography, "Talk about Venice," she said. Then she added, "Have you been to Venice?"

"Yes," I answered.

"What did you say?" She was angry.

"Yes," I repeated.

"Don't they teach you manners in your home?"

I was silent.

"Don't they teach you to answer, 'Yes, ma'am'?"

"No," I answered.

"No, ma'am!" she snapped, and I could see a strange happiness in her eyes. Later, I understood it was revenge.

After the exams we left for the seaside.

2 am ten years old. I am going to school. Maria Sole, Cristiana, and Giorgio are still studying at home. Everything is black. It's dark outside like thick soup, cold fog tickles your throat. The electric light goes on in the middle of the room. We rush to the bathroom, brush our teeth, put on our clothes laid out the night before on the chair (black woolen knickers under the dark blue sailor skirt, black woolen socks up to the knee). The maid brushes my hair and ties it with a black bow; my hair blows up around my shoulders crinkly and curly and golden and covers the collar of my sailor blouse. My black school satchel is full of books prepared last evening: exercise books, dictionary, fountain pen, ruler, half of the books on one side, half on the other. In the space left in the middle I slide a white shiny parcel which is brought with the breakfast in the dining room. We drink down the hot milk, munch the toast and butter and jam sitting politely around the table. Then we put on our dark blue sailor coats, Miss Parker is ready with her hat and coat on, and together we walk down the street to the Ginnasio Liceo D'Azeglio.

The satchel is very heavy. My hand carrying it gets very cold. Some kind of daylight begins to appear as I run into school. My brother Gianni goes in through the boys' entrance on Via San Quintino. He disappears and we will meet again at twelve o'clock when Miss Parker picks us up in front of the door where she has just left me.

Most of the children come alone, some are accompanied by their mothers, some by maids. A few, the daughters of officers, are met by soldiers who are the *attendenti* of their fathers. The maids, the *attendenti*, sometimes even the mothers carry the children's satchels. "Shameful," says Miss Parker. Some children are brought in cars driven by chauffeurs; Miss Parker considers this very vulgar. Even in the worst storm, snow or rain, we would never be allowed to go to school in a car.

We sit in an ugly, sad classroom, ten or twelve girls sitting together in a class of thirty boys, black pinafores covering our clothes. Classes are boring and anonymous. They consist of the teacher's calling a student to the desk and hearing the lesson he was given to study at home, then scribbling a secret mark onto the class copybook. Each holds his breath until the name of the chosen student is called out and then relaxes into nonlistening until the questioning is finished. The time dedicated to actual teaching or explaining or reading or communicating between teacher and pupils is as brief as possible. It is a relationship based on the menace of that little mark written down in that mysterious copybook.

At ten o'clock there is a break. All the girls go to a squalid, big, empty room at both ends of which is a dirty, stinking toilet. The smell pervades the big anteroom in which one is allowed to stand eating one's snack during those ten minutes of interval. The girls look with envy at my little white parcel, a white-bread sandwich filled with white butter and white chicken which I loathe. I look with envy at their coarse bread with two slices of spicy salami or a slab of *castagnaccio* or at the bread and chocolate they carry. In time I learn to barter my snack for theirs.

Then classes go on in the same monotonous boredom until the twelve-o'clock bell rings and we all rush down the stairs and into the gray street. Miss Parker is there waiting. We meet Gianni and we walk back home. I hate the classes, the homework, the lessons, the lack of interest or love. I hate the black.

Sometimes there is great excitement among the footmen. One of them walks around the house, the hall, up and down the marble staircase, the library, and the *saloni* carrying an iron palette full of flaming coals onto which he sprinkles a few drops of scent every ten footsteps. The perfumed smoke curls up around the tapestries and pictures and curtains. Vigiassa tells us that the Prince of Piedmont is coming for dinner and that our mother has given orders that we children should all be dressed alike, and in the hall downstairs ready to curtsy at the entrance of the royal couple. Our father and mother stand with us; Gianni in his sailor suit and we four sisters in embroidered muslin. My father is nervous because, as usual, my mother was not ready at the hour he had said she should be. My mother is beautiful.

Under the portico the car lights appear. The heavy door is swung open by Guglielmo, looking as handsome and grand as ever in his dark blue livery. The prince and princess walk in. They look like royalty ought to: he in uniform, smiling, she with a tiara and blue, dreamy eyes, both handsome and young and happy. We curtsy, they kiss us on the top of our heads. Then they walk up the stairs and we are sent to bed.

As we pass, we catch a glimpse of the men in tail coats with little ribbons and decorations on their left breast. Even Mario Garassino, the head butler, wears his decorations. He was very brave and was wounded during the war; the maids are very impressed. Before the guests arrived we had been allowed to look at the dining room, the beautiful lace tablecloth, the flowers, the vermeil sweet-holders full of chocolates and mints and fondants, the many glasses, the flowery china, the florist's girls running up and down handing a branch to their Madama Asinari as she puts a final touch to the decoration. A maid stands in a corner with a hot iron in her hand waiting to iron out a small crease in the tablecloth when at last these people will have left.

*O*r it is my grandfather, the Senatore, coming for dinner who makes the whole household nervous. He usually comes alone, without my grandmother; she is almost perpetually sick, lying in her bed without any special ailment, saying nasty things about everyone and being spoiled and fretted over by her husband and her son.

The Senatore's visit fills everybody with fright. Few people are invited to dine with him. I think he disapproves of my parents' friends and life. He arrives very punctually and walks up the stairs; my father walks out to the top of the staircase to meet him. They greet formally; my mother rushes into the library from a side door; my father sends her an angry glance, she is late again. *"Come stai, Senatore?"* She smiles at my grandfather; he looks at her and, fascinated by her charm, smiles back. At last.

My parents usually have cocktails served to their guests; my grandfather only drinks vermouth. Dinner is announced almost immediately. The decorations, the food, the table-cloth are different from the other parties; an understatement. We have just walked in to say good-night before the guests move in to the dining room. My grandfather is not very interested in our presence. My father looks embarrassed, my mother looks slightly bored. The Senatore does not come very often.

Sometimes on Saturday nights we are invited for dinner at our grandparents' house; it is a villa with a garden, the windows of the bedrooms look onto the Valentino Park. Our cousins are there and a few old family friends or distant relations. The women are all dressed in dark colors; black or purple or bottle green crepe de Chine long-sleeved *chemisiers*. My grandmother wears a little white and gray fur cape around her thin shoulders. She eats special food: little portions of yoghurt or a minute hashed steak, two spoonfuls of spinach purée, a mashed candied apricot. She eats her food with grimaces of loathing trying to explain to us how much she dislikes it all. In the meantime we are served rich, tasty *fritti misti* and *cassate* that the Neapolitan cook excels in. We love the food, so different from what we get at home, and the white, rather sweet wine that, here, we are allowed to taste. When dinner is over, coffee is served in the living room and my grandfather usually takes two or three of the men to a small study to have a serious talk. In the meantime my grandmother murmurs, "Isn't she ugly? Her mouth looks like a violin full of strings and things," pointing to some unfortunate wife who smiles politely back as she does not know what is being said. My grandmother always sees the worst of everybody and, with an amusing and nasty sense of humor, immediately points it out. She retires to go to bed early, and everyone goes home pretty soon after she has left.

Going there for dinner is a great change—the atmosphere is less chic, and there is no governess.

1933. I am eleven years old, Mussolini is coming to Turin. They are going to have an enormous *adunàta*, a meeting of all the schoolchildren in their Fascist uniforms doing a gym display at the stadium and then a parade across the middle of the town in military fashion. I love it. I love the singing until I am asked by the teacher to open my mouth and not sing because I am too out of tune to be tolerable. The *adunata* is the one time in which we are allowed to walk around the town alone, take a tram, wander around with our school friends, eat messy oily *bomboloni*, and arrive home at whatever hour of the day.

Nobody knows when and where the *adunata* is going to end, and it is impossible for Miss Parker to meet us. It is my first taste of freedom!

My father also wears a Fascist uniform. He looks at himself in the mirror and roars with laughter. For days afterward he endlessly describes the Turin ladies in their ridiculous uniform caps and soldier-like black suits, swooning at the idea of being on the same balcony with the Duce. My father has inherited from his mother a great sense of ridicule. My grandfather only shakes his head about all this nonsense.

I am a very good "piccola Italiana." They give me a decoration on a podium in the middle of the Piazza Statuto. The Federale of Turin pins a white-and-blue cross on my breast. I still don't know why. I am vaguely proud. My friends who are looking on from the windows of the Piazza tell me the only thing you can see is a pyramid of blond hair with a little round black beret on top.

I don't remember my mother in a Fascist uniform. When her seventh child is born, the Fascist party offers her a card which entitles her to free rides on all tramways; my mother is delighted with it even if she never has and never will ride in a tram. The idea enchants her and she carries it proudly.

My idea, then, of fascism is of something inevitable and ludicrous, but we don't hear much talk about it.

There are special shops where one buys the uniforms and the braid that you add on, or grades on your sleeves, small badges that indicate this corps or that corps of the *balilla*, the young Fascists, which you belong to. "Just fancy," says Miss Parker, "all the poor people who have to spend their money on this nonsense. Tch, tch," she says disapprovingly and shaking her head from one side to the other.

In the summer we went to Forte dei Marmi. The house had a garden with pine trees all the way to the beach. You walked through on the gravel path, opened the green wooden gate, and straight on, ahead of the flat sand dunes covered in light greeny blue ferns, was the sea. A sweet, mild, dreamy, silver-colored sea, with calm, bubbly waves that broke onto the clearest, finest sand. Little crabs ran up and down on the fringe of the water. A fisherman with a wooden tripod-like instrument sifted the sand near the shore and brought out tiny *arselle* in their multicolored shells which he then poured into a sack. The *arselle*, put into boiling water, opened and cleaned, made the best spaghetti sauce in the world. In the kitchen they hated the hours it took to prepare a cupful of sauce.

In the morning, early, when our father was there, he had us woken up and took us for a walk on the beach. We stopped and watched the fishermen pulling in the nets. They stood in two rows holding onto the ropes and shouting, "Oh, issa," as they pulled together, throwing their shoulders back and stepping slowly away from the sea. They coiled the rope at the top and walked back to the front of the row to start pulling again. At last the net appeared. You could feel it boiling and breathing even before you could see it, full of fish: jellyfish, long, thin *aguglie* with a pointed snout, flat soles, red *scorfani*, cuttlefish throwing out their black ink, sometimes a starfish. I was fascinated by the light, the life, the smell, the beauty. My father asked a fisherman to bring some small fish home and we ate it, fried, for breakfast. Of course Miss Parker disapproved; it would spoil our appetite for lunch.

There were two big tents on the beach, one for the grownups and one for the children. Miss Parker made us lie down in the sun, ten minutes on our stomach, ten minutes on our back, and that's all. For some strange reason she must have got it wrong because every year we were completely sunburned; at least I was. Gianni's skin seemed to get black the moment he walked into the sun, Clara's skin was bad anyway, and Maria Sole and Cristiana were under some second governess's jurisdiction. In the evening my shoulders ached. Vigiassa came in as soon as Miss Parker had gone to bed and covered my skin with beaten egg white.

We built sand castles and volcanoes and enormous tracks on which we raced marbles that you pushed along with a flick of your middle fingernail. When Miss Parker was not looking, we also built *trabocchetti*, booby traps, and over the hole we put a piece of newspaper which was then covered with sand. We hoped somebody would fall into it. Nobody did.

When there were many friends, we had a sand-castle contest. Two brothers, Emilio and Puccio Pucci, were the leaders because they were the eldest. Puccio was small, black and Mediterranean looking, everyone liked him. Emilio was tall, thin as a skeleton, with the long, sad face of a horse. Nobody wanted to be on his team. Miss Parker murmured, "Now, Suni, be a good little girl and ask to be on Emilio's team." I agreed and Puccio's castle was always the best.

At eleven thirty Miss Parker would say, "You can go in now," and we rushed into the sea. We waded out, we learned to swim. When the sea was rough we glided with the waves lying on wooden boards. At ten to twelve Miss Parker waved a handkerchief and the *bagnino* who accompanied us shouted, *"Fuori, fuori, è ora!"* If we pretended not to see or hear, or if we waited five minutes more, the next day we were not allowed to bathe.

$\mathcal{M}$y cousins were motherless and fatherless. Their mother, my grandparents' only daughter, died when her fifth son, Emanuele, was born. Of her death I remember only a great commotion in the house, crowds of people walking in and out of all the rooms. I heard that my grandmother was shattered. I think it is from then on that she spent most of her time in bed. All bad news was kept from her. When one of my cousins had to have her appendix out, my grandmother was told she had gone for a short trip to Rome and had had her called on the telephone from the hospital with somebody pretending to be the operator in between. I am sure my grandmother knew all the time what was really going on, but not having to admit it made it easier for her. I think she was very selfish. My father went to pay her a visit every day of his life. She disliked my mother.

After my aunt died, her husband was completely discarded by the family. My grandfather got the court to grant him the *patria potestà* over his grandchildren, and their father was given an apartment in the same house in which they lived and he could see them once every two weeks. When he died I don't think many cried. Once more we were dressed in black and followed the coffin and the flowers. That's all.

My cousin Berta was exactly my age. We were great friends. Her pale green eyes squinted and she had to go to the oculist, who prescribed eyeglasses. Her hair was straight and fair. My grandfather said she was very ugly. She was very nervous whenever something excited her. If she was supposed to go to a party or leave on a trip, she threw up and had a headache. So they put her to bed and she could never do anything. She loved my mother passionately and called her Mammà. But my grandparents, who were Berta's guardians, didn't like her coming around to us much. She had a governess, Mademoiselle Berthalot, who came from the Valley of Pellice; a good, jolly common woman who spoke a terrible French patois. We called her Tolò.

When Berta and I were together we were continually scolded because we never stopped chatting and giggling. They said we talked nonsense. She didn't go to school because of her eyes.

My grandfather had had a chapel built on top of the hill where the cemetery stood in Villar Perosa, his country place. It was here also that he had built the RIV ball-bearing factory next to the road which ran at the bottom of the valley. Berta's mother was buried in the pale gray cold marble under the niches prepared for my grandfather and grandmother, their names already engraved in the stone.

One day we were taken up to the chapel. Berta knelt on the cold marble and suddenly I saw a big tear splash onto the stone floor. I was astonished. I had not been taught to throw my arms around her and hug her. I just went on kneeling in silence and felt terrible.

I did not know where Berta's father was buried.

*D*uring the Christmas holidays they took us skiing. We used to go to Saint Moritz, until my grandfather decided to build a winter resort with hotels and funiculars in the Alps above Turin. While they were building the strange tower-like hotel and the funiculars in Sestriere, we stayed in a dismal pension which had been there on the pass for years and years. We were made to climb the hills with sealskins under our skis. I hated this climbing and got tired out. My father said it was because I never stopped chattering with Berta and used up all my breath talking. I got cold, my hands and feet and ears almost froze. One day at the end of a long run I sat on the snow and cried. When they took me back to the pension I had a high temperature, and when we reached home in Turin I was covered with measle spots. I felt miserable. Years later I enjoyed being a good skier, but then it seemed only an ordeal.

Clara had the measles at the same time as I did, and we were sent to Rapallo to convalesce with an elderly nurse hired for the occasion. She would let us buy cakes in the shops and allowed us to beat an egg yolk with sugar for breakfast, then fill the cup with coffee and milk. It was a marvelous holiday. Spring was blooming on the Riviera, the air was sweet and full of smells—flowers and sea and fried fish.

Going back to the fog of Turin was a nightmare.

*O*ur other grandmother is Princess Jane. She is American, tall, holds herself very straight. Her hair is white and beautiful. During the winter she wears a veil, black or gray, hanging from two crescents joining in a point on the top of her head. In the summer she wears white dresses down to the ground, white shoes and stockings, and carries a white parasol. My grandmother has a maid, Rosa, with whom she has the most awful rows, one antagonist speaking American English and the other answering in the worst Romanaccio. My father pulls Princess Jane's leg because he says she is always talking and quarreling about money, like all Americans.

Princess Jane, who is the widow of Carlo Bourbon del Monte, Prince of San Faustino, adores people and parties and gossip and the strange mix-ups of life. She says atrocious things at which shy people tremble, but she can make anyone's life fun if she decides to look after them. They say she drank terribly after she was widowed, until she fell in love with Axel Munthe, who asked her to stop. From that day on she never drank anything but water.

At Easter time we are taken to Rome and Princess Jane gives a party for us with all the elegant children of the capital. They are mostly princes and princesses.

"How can you, Virginia, dress your children so badly?" my grandmother observes us, horrified. "They look like grocers' daughters dressed in green velvet."

"Stop it, Mamah!" My mother is furious.

Our party is a desperate battle to overcome the horror of looking like grocers' daughters. The Roman children don't talk to us anyway. They all speak Italian with an English accent and don't understand how anybody could live in Turin. They live in beautiful *palazzi* with terraced gardens, where their Easter eggs are hidden. They don't go to school; they go for picnics to the Villa Doria. The girls are all called Donna Topazia or Donna Babù or Donna Francesca. We are called by our names.

*T*his summer, 1935, they have decided to send Clara for a tour in Austria with some *Gräfin* to accompany her. Gianni must repeat all his exams in September because of his very bad conduct in school. This is a measure very rarely adopted in Italian schools, but it can be done at the *preside's* discretion as a punishment. It means practically no holidays. But Gianni throws his schoolmates' satchels onto passing trucks so that they have to run after them for miles; he laughs; he is rude to teachers in front of the school door; he needs a lesson. When the news comes, nobody dares tell my father. I am made to dine in bed at night because I am so thin and I get nosebleeds. I am lying there with the tray on my knees when my father comes in to say hello. I tell him that Gianni has been *rimandato* for his conduct. He can't believe it. He is furious, he rushes off to look for Gianni. I lie there terrified. I have already cried my eyes out in school. "Why do you cry?" the other girls say. "They'll scold your brother, not you." They don't understand. Nobody understands that it means spending the holidays without him. He is my friend, we are so near in age.

We go out on a boat together and the sailors of the yachts that anchor off the beach at Forte dei Marmi give us tips as we carry them to the shore and then they see us come back all dressed up when our parents visit the owners. We bicycle to the village and eat ice-cream cones at the *Glacia*, where the boys let us hold the long wooden paddle while the ice cream is made as the machine swirls around.

I help Gianni push his car up the hill in Villar Perosa and sit on the back of it as we scoot down, he at the wheel. We don't need to talk much to each other. We understand.

We are now in Forte dei Marmi but it has been decided that from tomorrow, July 15, Gianni will go to my grandfather's house in Villar Perosa with a tutor and God knows how many teachers to give him lessons all day long.

My father has come to Forte dei Marmi for the weekend. Princess Jane is there, too. My mother is in France taking a cure. It is Sunday. Our father walks with us to Mass which is said in the open air in a garden under the trees.

When we come home there is an aeroplane circling. It

alights on the sea in front of our strip of beach, where the tents are. They row a *patino* out toward it and return with Ferrarin waving from the seat. Ferrarin is the hero pilot of Italy and a great friend of my father's. He takes me and then Gianni for a short flight. It is our first taste of an aeroplane.

Then we are all sitting at lunch together. My father is gay, they are talking aeroplanes. "With a Fiat plane and Ferrarin as a pilot, I am ready to fly anywhere," he says.

Gianni leaves by train with the butler, my father will fly to Genoa and meet him in Turin.

The sunlight is still out after dinner and Miss Parker has allowed a few girls from neighboring houses to come and play for a short time. Strangely, I am very happy and gay. I am wearing a cotton dress with red poppies all over it. We run around among the pine trees, we dance on the pine needles holding hands.

The telephone rings. Princess Jane hates the telephone; somebody calls me in to help her. She stands in the corner of the room holding the receiver to her ear. She can't understand what they are saying. Then I see her open her eyes wide and sway slightly backward. She looks at me and murmurs, "Suni, your father is dead."

I remember taking a train with Princess Jane, my younger sisters, the governesses, the maids. I remember people getting on the train at different stations. Everybody cried, said, "Why? Why?"

"It is not possible. He was so young." For me, at thirteen, my father at forty-three seemed very old.

"All those children."

"Poor Senatore."

Princess Jane, speechless, but now and then she would sigh, "Virginia, Virginia."

The accident had been so stupid. The plane had alighted and was taxiing across the water of the port of Genoa when it struck a log and capsized. My father, who was half-standing to get out of the plane, had had his head cut open by the propeller at the back of the cockpit. He died instantly. Ferrarin, who was sitting down, was uninjured, not a scratch; he was in severe shock. I don't think he ever recovered completely.

My grandfather, informed that his son had had an accident, had driven to the hospital in Genoa, asked to see the patient Agnelli, and had been answered by somebody at the desk that he could go to the mortuary chapel. He walked in, looked at his dead son, his only son, for ten minutes in silence, then drove back to Turin.

At the station, in Turin, there were more people. The *portone* of the house was semi-shut and covered in black draperies as was the mourning custom of the time. The house was a stream of people walking up and down the stairs, in and out, everywhere. In the red *salone* next to the dining room, in a wooden coffin, lay my father with a bandage around his head. There were nuns praying and candles and flowers and heat and so many people. Gianni was sitting alone in a bedroom, the floor covered with newspapers. Then friends started coming in, everybody kissed you, hugged you, cried.

My mother lay on her bed. She was evidently disturbed by all the people. She looked totally lost. She made me think of a sick animal inside a cage.

The next day was the funeral. In the morning they said Mass in the house. At that time, unless you had a special permission from the Cardinal, you could only say Mass in a private house if a prince of the Royal family was present. The Duke of Aosta came, tall, tall, so good-looking, very sad. The Prince of Piedmont was the godfather of my youngest brother, only eight months old, named Umberto after him. The prince visited. We were there, standing, all dressed in black, all the time. Aunts and relatives, and old women and men of all kinds, and friends from all over the place—shocked, horrified, curious, desperate. My father must have been loved.

First they took the hearse to the church around the corner from our house in Turin, but there were so many people they had to walk up the Corso Oporto on one side and down the other so that they could all follow in procession.

We walked in a row just behind the hearse pulled by horses—Clara, Gianni, myself, Maria Sole, and Cristiana. My brother Giorgio was only five so he was kept home with Umberto. It was stifling hot. I sweated in the silk long-sleeved black dress. The smell of the gardenias in the undulating flower wreath stuck in the boiling air. *"Por cit,"* said the Turinese women in dialect as we walked slowly past the crowd lining the street.

Then, after the service, we sat in a car with our mother, who had not walked with us, and drove up to Villar Perosa where my father was to be buried. My mother wore a black veil all around her face. She held me on her lap and now and then squeezed my arms so tightly I almost cried out in pain.

At Villar my grandfather was waiting in the garden. He walked toward my mother with her children gathered around her. He stopped and stood mute, tears were streaming down his face. "You mustn't, Senatore, you mustn't," my mother cried out desperately. He shook his head and walked away.

My grandmother did not appear. They stopped the church bells from ringing so that she would not hear them tolling for her son.

They put my father into another one of those gray marble niches. His name was not engraved on it yet.

We went back, thank God, to Forte dei Marmi. We wore white shorts and white blouses, white sandals. As long as everything was white it was all right, so long as you didn't mix white with black. We wore black bathing suits.

Princess Jane came with us. She was worried and bad-tempered. She sat under the grownups' tent alone with her parasol and got bored stiff. Miss Parker came up with a camera and asked, "Would you like me, Princess Jane, to take a snapshot of you with the children?"

She stamped her foot on the sand. "I can't think of anything," she declared, "that I would hate more."

Miss Parker retired meekly to the children's tent.

A man walked down the beach every morning. They said he was a writer, an anti-Fascist, living in Forte dei Marmi *al confino*. That meant he could not leave and had to report to the police every day. He had a strange white dog on a leash, a thin, sleek, lamblike-looking dog bred on the island of Lipari where they kept the politically undesirable.

Princess Jane told the *bagnino* to go and tell that man that she wanted to talk to him. She was getting lonesome and had no desire to talk about the bourgeois problems or joys of the people who owned houses around us. They usually had lots of children and not much imagination.

So the man walked up the stretch of dry sand, which got very hot in the sun, squeezing his eyes against the light.

"Aren't you Malaparte? Come here," Princess Jane addressed him, "I want you to talk to me. You are very good-looking."

He was, in a strange exotic way. He had straight black hair, shining like velvet, brushed back on a very round head. His lashes were a thick frame around his dark shiny eyes, as if they were part of his glance. When he smiled, his lips curled inside and disappeared, his teeth were white and animal-like. He was covered from head to foot in some kind of oil and his armpits were shaved. He laughed, a sad cruel laugh, then he sat in the sun and entertained Princess Jane, who sat in the shade. He was a fascinating entertainer.

Then my mother came back. She was beautiful, frail, thirty-five years old, the practically penniless mother of seven children who would one day inherit a large fortune.

She loved life and laughter, was totally uneducated, wrote Italian with all sorts of spelling mistakes, was astonishingly generous to friends and strangers. She was fundamentally and always a girl. I came to think of her as if she were my daughter. I wanted to protect her; I wanted her to be happy. I froze with terror every time she went away, when I thought that she, too, might die.

She loved the sea. We bathed for hours together, morning and afternoon, forgetting Miss Parker's rules. We went for long, long walks on the damp sand near the sea, past the pier of Forte dei Marmi, toward the Ronchi, picking shells, paddling in the waves, looking at the crabs and the water fleas jumping up and down in a mad dance. We had lunch on the beach under the tent and lay in the sun or the shade—wherever we liked.

I loved everything about my mother. Her wet chestnut, reddish hair drying in the sun, the freckles that appeared on her skin when she stayed in the open air, her smell, like a bowl of milk.

Malaparte came again to talk to Princess Jane on the beach. He looked at my mother intensely. He sat and talked about himself, the war (he had run away from school when he was fifteen to join up), his Liceo Cicognini in Tuscany, the dozens of duels he had fought, his meetings with Mussolini, the prison, the island of Lipari. Whatever he talked about became a marvelous story. I could listen to him forever, and forever he could go on talking.

Malaparte lived in a stone house shut off from the road by thick bushes of oleanders, green and damp. From a small arched terrace on the first floor you could see the beach and the sea. Malaparte told us about a strange boy who had come to stay with him. He described the boy, unwashed and limping, the way he wrote, lying in bed, covering all the sheets in ink spots to the great fury of the *guardiana*, Maria. The boy, aggressively shy, was Moravia.

Sometimes my mother would take us to Malaparte's house. We sat in the almost unfurnished room and he gave us Malvasia, a thick golden sweet wine from Lipari, to drink. Then he told us stories. We sat on the floor and listened, until he put his hand on my mother's head and pulled her hair and laughed at her and we would take our bicycles and go home. I was slightly drunk and very happy, thinking about my mother who had stayed on with him.

Or we would go to Viareggio and dine at the Buon Amico, eating little fried fish and *peperoni* and complicated, tasty, unhealthy food that would have made Miss Parker despair. The girls who waited on the table were sisters, their mother was in the kitchen. They all chatted with the clients incessantly, suggesting they eat this or that, carrying in a spoonful of *caciucco* to taste or a biscuit filled with anis seed. It was hot, friendly, and happy.

In the afternoon we would bicycle up to the Cinquale where Dazzi, the sculptor, had his house and studio. He would let us play with the clay he worked with and climb over the enormous slabs of white marble that he was sculpting. We all posed as models for him, and he made two big bronze doors with the figures of us on them for the chapel my grandfather was having built in Sestriere dedicated to Sant' Edoardo in memory of my father.

It was an unexpected madhouse. Dazzi shouted, his white-haired companion made *castagnaccio* with nuts in it; people came and went, models or friends, marble workers, visitors, artists.

The time came when we had to go back to Turin and school.

When I go to Turin now, as I look at the hills on the other side of the river, the trees and the green, as I walk through the Piazza San Carlo with its elegant arches, I think: It is true. Turin is an elegant town as people say. Then, I only saw its gray squalor. Then, my world was restricted to the few streets down which we walked to go to school or for our afternoon walks. Then, Piazza Statuto was where they had a very good food shop that sold the best cheese and Piazza Carignano was next to the bookshop that sent my father books. I never realized they were beautiful. They were piazzas. It is now that I discover there are fruit trees and flowers and cherries and narrow, winding roads that climb to the Collina from which you look out at the Alps. It is now that the old houses and courtyards and streets attract me.

At school my teacher had changed. Now I had a man teacher, dirty, ordinary, uninterested in his class. He picked his nose and at recess said, "Who wants to go and shit may now leave for ten minutes." I was shocked. I hated him as much as he disliked me. My marks were a disaster.

My grandfather had a projection room built in the basement of our house so that we could look at movies (we were not allowed, being in mourning, to go out to the cinema).

At the end of the children's corridor, there was the gymnasium, where every evening after we had finished our homework a teacher came to make us exercise and then play basketball. A few friends, boys and girls, joined us. It was the only hour of the day I really looked forward to. After gym we would sit and talk while the boys and girls changed their shoes before they went home. Some kind of friendship was born. If one of them was sick and did not appear, we rang up and asked about him. At times we would meet in Sestriere and go skiing together. But still we did not belong.

My cousin Berta was living with her sister Laura, who was married to a young, curly-haired, charming boy. They produced a baby every year. Laura was forever knitting, talking about nannies and carrot juice and fresh air for the children. Her husband, Giancarlo, worked at Fiat. He was the one man left in the whole family who could work with my grandfather. My cousin Giovanni and my brother Gianni were both still in school.

Giancarlo, Laura, and her younger brothers and sisters lived in a seventeenth-century house with a courtyard and garden. A curved white staircase opened into a round entrance hall from which you entered into *saloni* and *salottini* at the end of which was a stuccoed dining room, lively, colored, gay. The ceiling was lined with mirrors and Compagnie des Indes porcelain.

Once every fortnight we went there for a cooking lesson in a small kitchen upstairs. Clara, Berta, and myself cooked. We were allowed to invite Gianni, Giovanni, and Lodovico, our only real childhood friend, to eat the food we had prepared. Our teacher was sweet; she gave *economia domestica* classes in a girls' school. Her one worry was not to spend money. Her meals were very cheap and quite inedible. Her favorite was tunafish mousse with a few shreds of salad covered in ready-made mayonnaise. We kept a book and wrote down the price of the finished meal, adding the costs of gas, electricity, and water through a complicated accounting system.

Then the teacher left. We threw the food out and ate the sandwiches that the boys brought in their pockets. We drank red wine and talked: Giovanni told us about how much he was in love; Gianni was skeptical; Lodovico made amusing remarks.

A few months later Giovanni sat with us and was very sad. He said that last Sunday, while he was skiing in fresh powder snow down an empty slope among the trees, he had suddenly realized that for ten minutes he had not been thinking about his love. It meant he wasn't so much in love any more; it meant that something was beginning to change. As he talked he fiddled aimlessly with a knife. It slipped and he cut his finger deep. The blood dripped onto the table, the floor. He looked at it covering his hand, flowing out of him. He just sat there without moving until we bandaged him up.

One afternoon a strange thing happened, and when it happened, we discovered that we had pretended we were not afraid of the storm. Now the clouds were bursting.

A law officer at the door insisted on seeing my mother to hand over to her, personally, the paper he was carrying. My mother refused to receive him. Pasquale, the butler, kept on repeating that Donna Virginia was not at home. The officer insisted he knew that Donna Virginia was at home. In the end, Pasquale signed for the warrant himself and assured the officer that he would give it to Donna Virginia when he could get in touch with her. The officer left; Pasquale brought the paper to my mother's room. It was an injunction by the judge ordering my mother to leave the house immediately. She would be allowed to see her children once every two weeks for forty-eight hours, outside of their house. The *patria potestà* over her children had been given to their grandfather, Senatore Agnelli.

My mother's indignation rose as the minutes went by. She called a few lawyers on the telephone, asked them to obtain a meeting for her with Mussolini, and sent the seven of us to put on our coats. We drove off like mad in two cars and at the station in Alessandria we boarded a train for Rome. We sat, all of us together, in a compartment, feeling and behaving like refugees. My mother was nervous and afraid; now and then she would cry. We didn't know what to do to comfort her. Clara kept on nudging at me and saying, "Do something. You know we'll never see Mammà again."

The train came into the Genoa station, we put the lights out and shut the compartment door. Nothing happened. Then the train pulled slowly out of the station. A few minutes later the train stopped again, this time in open countryside. Men came aboard. They walked up and down the carriages looking into every compartment. They came to ours, they put on the light, one of the men addressed my mother:

"In what quality are you traveling, Signora?"

"What do you mean, 'In what quality'?" My mother was shaking.

"I mean, what kind of a family is this?"

"A mother and her seven children."

"I see."

He beckoned to the other men that he had found what he was looking for.

"You had better get off the train. You understand, Signora, that under the circumstances, these children are being kidnaped."

Then he turned to us. "Please don't shout or make a scene; it will only make things worse for your mother."

They marched us off the train holding us tightly by both wrists, one policeman on each side.

My mother went to Rome alone. I was too stunned, too tired, too hurt to be able to say a word.

They took us to the hotel and next morning they drove us back to Turin.

*M*iss Parker was her dear, darling, usual self—behaving as if nothing had happened, comforting in her British uninvolvement. She took no sides, judged no one. She did her duty, and that was to bring up children and teach them manners.

But the other governesses, there were two or three others at the moment, were revolting. They couldn't take our mother's side for fear of losing their job; yet they felt they might alientate us forever, and that they didn't like. So they tried to play up to us, offering little favors, saying half-phrases to hear our reaction, telling us the Senatore was a really great man and loved us very much.

I don't remember my grandfather coming to see us. I think our silent hostility rather surprised him. He was unexpectedly struck by the fact that people could care for one another. We went there for lunch. We were polite and icy.

He sat, as always, at the head of the table with an empty, deep plate in front of him. At the side was a special cutting instrument that, in Italy, is used to slice truffles, and a dish with clean, whole fresh vegetables: one tomato, one celery, one fennel, one artichoke. He slowly sliced one vegetable after the other into the plate, then added salt and pepper, and poured oil over the salad. It was his meal. Every day at lunchtime he prepared his own salad and ate it slowly while he drank a glass of Punt e Mes vermouth and listened to songs on the radio.

He sliced his artichoke and tomato with great care. His pale blue eyes smiled peacefully. We were still polite and icy. After lunch we left. He would go to his room and lie on the bed covering himself with his jacket in the military fashion, a habit he had learned when he was an officer in the cavalry. After a twenty-minute sleep he would go back to Fiat.

My mother engaged the best Roman lawyers; not all were prepared to accept. It was not easy to fight my grandfather at that time in Italy. He was powerful and hard and accustomed to having his own way.

Mussolini agreed to see her. She told him she was being mistreated. She was a widow with seven children and Mussolini should not accept that, in a country ruled by him, she should be deprived of her children because she had a lover.

Mussolini saw her point. He liked her battling nature and liked acting the magnanimous, all-powerful giant.

He also liked the idea of giving advice to my grandfather. He got my grandfather to withdraw his claim. My mother said she would stop seeing Malaparte. He had been, for a short time, editor of *La Stampa*, the newspaper my grandfather owned. He was described as an *avventuriero*. I don't know if he was fired or if he left, but after one more duel he was no longer editor of *La Stampa*. Mussolini had very much impressed my mother. My grandfather was impressed by her determination.

My mother came back home. She was sad. She tried to pretend she wasn't. She invited people for lunch and dinner and now we all had our meals together—guests, children, tutors, governesses—an enormous, crazy table.

Lotti, a girl whose family had been very friendly with my parents, came and stayed with us. Her age was in between our mother's and ours. She wrote letters for my mother and acted as companion, friend, secretary, housekeeper, and person-in-charge when my mother left Turin. Mammà knew she could rely on her to always tell her the truth.

Poor Lotti, she listened to everyone's confidential troubles, she knew the secrets of every person in the house, they all told her their grievances, sadnesses, problems. She was supposed to tell a governess that she ought to wash her hair more often and the tutor to talk less when there were guests at the dinner table. My mother pestered her, woke her up in the middle of the night to discuss some ridiculous detail, and told her it was her fault when anything went wrong.

y mother had fallen in love with a house in Rome. It was the Academy of the Arcadia, founded by Queen Christina of Sweden. Mammà managed to get the old poets who ran the academy to rent the house to her for thirty years. She would tell us about it: it had a garden on different levels, a double round staircase winding through it, a fountain, an enormous pine tree, and an amphitheater that faced the front of the house, covered by a wistaria that climbed to the terrace on top. Inside was a round room like a *battistero,* and a church-looking high *salone* with the ceiling covered in stucco. The steep stairway led upstairs to one big bedroom with a terrace, which was my mother's, and a few incredibly small rooms with bunk beds. Every room was on a different floor with steps going from one to the other. The view was not to be believed. Rome lay at your feet, golden, warm, remote, beautiful. *"Dimmi ancora, Mammà"*—I would sit at the bottom of her bed—"tell me more of the house and the flowers and the light and the *tramontana* blowing leaves in the blue sky."

She hated Turin so much. People criticized her because she walked into the street without wearing a hat, or used the most awful language with the most angelic smile, or refused to listen to the nasty gossip of the old, ugly Turinese ladies.

The one thing that interested her was a nursing school in the San Vito Hospital on the hills overlooking Turin. She founded it, named it after my father, and was passionately involved with it. At Christmas she took us to her nursing school for a ceremony, and afterward someone asked us to distribute oranges and sweets to the sick people. I came home and was ill; I could not stand the smell of sickness.

I went riding with my cousin Berta. We galloped in the fields chattering away, as usual. When we came to a ditch, I shouted, "Ditch!" and Berta lowered her hands and let her horse jump. Without her glasses she couldn't see a thing and they wouldn't let her ride with her glasses on. She was exceptionally brave and we had a lovely time. I loved the fields full of poppies, the thin white beech-tree woods, the streams one suddenly came upon from an embankment.

*T*hen, one day, it was spring. My mother couldn't stand Turin any longer and she took us all to Rome.

The flowers were out on the trees in the streets and the wistaria on the terrace was bursting into pale mauve bunches. Little green buds were almost creeping into the room when you opened the window in the morning. Sleeping, four of us together, in bunks that filled the room was, for me, the height of bliss.

We went to school at a nun's private institute near the Via Veneto. It was clean and painted in pastel colors; there were few children and the teachers were friendly and kind. I got such *fou rires* with another girl in class that they would send us outside, into the corridor, until we had stopped laughing.

In the afternoon we walked on the Gianicolo, which was just above our house. At the end of the road there were grass-covered stairs. At the top was the fountain with water falling through three wide arches and the gate that opened onto the park. The sunsets were red. The whole town was flaming. It was so unbearably beautiful I thought my heart would stop beating.

Mammà was happy. Her friends came and laughed with her, they kissed her when they walked in. They were so different from the Turinese who only kissed you when somebody died. Maids served at the table, wearing colored aprons and shawls. The guests pinched them and they squealed. I could not believe that life could be so completely different. Here, everybody wanted to have a good time. The one thing that they took seriously was their love affairs.

School meant meeting one's friends and joking between one class and another. I began actually to enjoy the classes, to understand that learning could be interesting. They didn't ask me to write an essay about some boring, incomprehensible sonnet; they read poetry aloud and made me like it. The nuns smiled when they met you in the corridor and asked you how you were getting along. I was astonished.

The crowded dirty streets of Trastevere, the river with its high bridges always full of people, the ruins, the palaces, the language, the happy rude laughter, even the churches made me feel alive. Before, I felt alive only when I was skiing, sailing, or riding.

Little black-haired men swarmed into the house. They cut the telephone wires. They presented my mother with a piece of paper. This time, the house being hers, it was her children who were going to be taken back to Turin and handed over to their grandfather, who had become their legal guardian.

They put us in four cars full of policemen. I tried to jump out but it was useless, there were too many of them, they just held me.

At Civitavecchia we boarded the train for Turin.

Clara and I were asked to pay a visit to our grandmother. At seventeen and fifteen we were considered old enough to do so. She was lying in bed, as usual, looking bored and unhappy. She said she wanted to give each of us a fur coat as a present. We coldly answered we did not want a fur coat, "Thank you very much." She dismissed us almost immediately. The exchange of conversation was not brilliant.

After this visit I decided I was going to fight. I bought a series of knives that I hung on a belt around my waist. When one of the odious traitor-governesses began to talk to me I would open one of the knives and start playing with it. I could see the fright in her eyes and I rather enjoyed it.

I shouted in the middle of the courtyard, so that the neighbors in the houses across the wall could hear me, that I wanted my mother back. One morning my grandfather called me on the telephone. "Susanna," he said sternly (nobody ever called me anything but Suni), "if I hear you have made another scene, I will send you to boarding school!" "Thank you, Nonno," I answered. And that was the end of the conversation.

The real nightmare was my mother's visits to Turin every two weeks. She was not allowed to come to the house, so she stayed in an old, sad, ugly hotel across from the station. She talked all the time about lawyers and lawsuits and sentences and judges. We hung around the grayish sitting room. Some friends came to see my mother to show their loyalty but most people were afraid. We went for short walks. In town they turned around and looked at us; on the hills it was foggy and cold. It was like being in front of a patient's room in a hospital where he has been operated on and waiting for the verdict of the doctor who never appears. I ended up by wishing my mother wouldn't come at all—it would have been less hellish.

Between her visits we lived like always except that we became intolerable. We went to the perfume shop around the corner where, when we were small, they used to give us little samples of tooth paste and soaps and hand lotions that filled us with joy, and bought the biggest, most expensive bottle of French perfume in the shop, and gave it as a present to our cooking teacher. We still were never given money to carry with us but we went into the shops and charged. None of the governesses dared argue, afraid of how rudely we would answer back.

Clara sat at the window with a rose in her hair and made eyes at a boy who lived in the house across the street. She dropped notes to him in the street and finally managed to pretend she was visiting a school friend and went out in a car with him. I was so nervous that somebody would find out, that in the evening I had a fever.

We telephoned all the *pasticcerie* in Turin and ordered enormous trayfuls of cream pastries and chocolate candies to be sent to a hateful gym teacher whose classes we used to attend years before.

We spat from the balcony of the library onto the people who were passing on the sidewalk. Guglielmo, the porter, was insulted and cursed by serious, dark-clothed men going to their offices who appeared with a big spittle crawling down their arms. He apologized profusely, swore it couldn't have been us, and then talked to us in begging despair. We howled with laughter.

We ordered elaborate dinners from the cook and then refused to eat anything.

We sat locked up in the bathroom until past midnight talking, soaking in the tub, and drinking red wine we had stolen from the pantry.

We didn't study. We didn't make sense. We just contradicted everything.

It was late spring of 1937. The rows of horse chestnut trees that flanked the alley of the Corso Oporto were lusciously green, spotted with their white-and-pink flowers.

One judge in Rome had issued a decree in favor of my mother. There were more to come. It wasn't a definitive victory, but it was an opening, a possibility.

It seems nobody dared tell my grandfather. They lied to him until a friend of my mother's went to him and told him that his lawyers had lost. He was astonished. Gianni pleaded for our mother; then the Senatore gave up. He declared that if a woman was so loved by her children there must, by God, be something special in her.

Besides, he must have been getting rather worried about what would happen to us all if life went on the way it had during the last months. People were beginning to talk. My mother was not going to give up fighting, whatever happened, and, even in Fascist Italy, opinions still existed.

The Senatore invited us all to dinner with our mother and could not have been more charming and kind and sweet to her. My mother had already forgiven him.

"You are so beautiful," he said, "and young. And your children love you. I think you should all leave Italy for a while. Go, Virginia, and find a nice house on the French Riviera where you can enjoy yourselves for the summer. Have a nice holiday. It will be a change for the children, too."

When joy comes so suddenly, you don't have the time to taste it fully. I would have liked to have time to think of how marvelous it would all be.

It was there before I could think about it. And so, one forgets.

A house was found on Cap Martin, inside an enormous park that sloped down to the sea. It was a big house, falling to pieces in a charming fashion, with dozens of bedrooms, mosquito nets, corridors lined with flowery material, living rooms opening onto terraces and gardens, lots of furniture, and an air of old luxury. We arrived with maids and cooks and cars and chauffeurs and a holiday atmosphere.

I was only fifteen but I had learned to drive a car. I drove from morning to evening up and down the whole Riviera, from corniche to corniche, loving every drunken minute of it. We had friends stay with us, went swimming at the Monte Carlo beach, gambled at the slot machines, bought exotic food in the shops, lay in the sun, sat in the shade, went out at night, didn't change for dinner, didn't get up for breakfast, walked around without any clothes on, slept wherever at whatever time. There were boys talking to Clara about love and Clara listened. Gianni and the other boys went out with tarts. The little ones, as my brothers and sisters from Maria Sole downward were now always called, bathed and played under the pine trees. I took the car and drove for miles, stopping to look at a bright blue triangle of sea appearing between the silver-green bushes and the red earth, breathing the smell of the sun heating the salt water and flowers, enjoying the roads winding up the mountain, the villas encircled by tall trees, the sensation of nothingness which possessed me.

My mother went out a lot. All the men were in love with her. She threw back her little head and shook her rust-shadowed curls, laughing. We joked with her, made her smile, then irritated her by putting on the most revolting Piedmontese accent to talk to the people who came to pay her visits. We went shopping together, walking on the sunny paths of the Cap, swimming in other people's pools or off our beach.

Princess Jane came to stay. She was surprised at the total disorder of everything. Nobody knew who was going to be there for lunch or dinner, how many, at what time. Miss Parker tried to cope in some way by at least having a fixed timetable for the little ones' meals. Cars came and went, driven mostly by Gianni and myself, both without a license. Guests appeared with their suitcases out of nowhere. Different men came to take Mammà swimming somewhere down the coast.

We wore shorts up to our derrières and hair down to our derrières. We went around in crowds mostly, pulling everybody's leg. I don't think we were very popular.

We were certainly not popular with Princess Jane. She walked into one of the bedrooms one morning and found us all half-dressed, lying around. "What are you drinking?" she asked, horrified.

"Oh, this?" (We were rather blasé.) "Pineapple juice and champagne."

"Champagne? For breakfast?" She was beside herself.

"Why not? It's good," we answered.

She headed straight to my mother's room and from the door declared, "Virginia, you must have gone completely mad!"

Part Two

*Y*es, it was true, Mammà had said. Perhaps we were leading a rather eccentric life. She believed in always letting everyone do what they thought best. Life would teach them. But she admitted that a year in boarding school in England might be good for us, to show us how other people lived in 1937.

So we packed. Clara, whom I had practically always shared my life with, was to go to finishing school in London and I would be sent with Maria Sole to a convent at Saint Leonards-on-Sea. Cristiana would stay in Turin with Giorgio and Umberto and, of course, Gianni, who had to finish Italian school.

In England, Maria Sole and I shared an ice-cold room with two beds and a window that looked onto emptiness. Some idiotic girl would wake you up at six o'clock swinging a big bell up and down the corridor to tell you it was time to push yourself into a gray sweater and scratchy blue tunic to walk down to Mass.

The classes were small, the lessons totally childish. The nuns taught us what in Italy they taught you when you were nine years old and always as to an audience of half-wits. The intellectual level of the whole school was below zero. The nuns who taught were infantile and silly; the girls were worse.

After lunch we played lacrosse in a field or walked single-file down the streets of Saint Leonards. Sometimes you could see a cliff or a wave. Afterward, in one enormous hall, full of tables and benches, we did our homework. I put my head on the table and sobbed desperately. I just couldn't be throwing my life away like this. I had never felt a more devastating boredom; it was the one time in my life in which I thought I would go mad. "What is the matter, Susanna?" the nuns asked. "Are you homesick?"

"No, I am not homesick, I am bored. I have no one to

talk to. I want some boys around to discuss something with. I have nothing to do."

"Perhaps you might go to church and say a few prayers," they suggested. It was hopeless. We spoke different languages.

What killed me was that Maria Sole, who was never a very talkative person, seemed to be quite happy. I tortured her explaining how awful it all was, but she just looked at me in silence and went back to the book she was reading. One day I beat her with a brush.

I wrote letters by the hundreds saying I couldn't stand it and would go crazy. I rang up Clara in London and cried. She said I ought to think about Mammà and not make trouble.

The nuns read the letters I received and fainted. Who were all those boys writing to me? "My friends," I would say. "Isn't one supposed to have friends?" They looked at me with an uncomprehending, rather pathetic gaze.

They took away my books and gave me childish stories that I couldn't have read even if I had tried. They emptied my cupboard onto the floor so that I would learn to keep it more tidily. They loathed me. I loathed them, their denseness, their unreality, their lack of objectivity, their false secluded calm.

I went to the bathroom one afternoon, and Maria Sole came in with me. We were used to taking a bath with six or seven of us in the same bathroom. A livid nun was waiting for us outside. "You dirty, disgusting girls," she hissed, "aren't you ashamed of yourselves! What are you doing in there, the two of you together?"

I could have slapped her face; this was too much for me. I went downstairs, called my mother on the telephone, and told her I was leaving. If she didn't come and take me away, I would run away, kill myself, and she would never see me

again. Vaguely Mammà tried to argue with me. "No," I
said, "no, I won't stay here. I don't care what happens to
me. Anything is better than this hypocritical asylum for
idiots."

She arrived; six nuns sat severely around a table; she was
received; then I was called in. I opened the door, looked at
my mother being very serious—totally incongruous in that
monstrous setting—caught her eye, winked at her, and
started to laugh. She laughed back; the nuns couldn't
understand what was going on.

We left at once. Still, Maria Sole didn't seem to care.

We stayed together in a suite at Claridge's and
looked for another school for me. The one thing Mammà
would not accept was that I should be in the same place as
Clara; she didn't want me to forget that I was two years
younger.

At finishing schools they thought I was too young; at
boarding schools they thought I was too grown up. Finally,
at Queen's Gate, we found something—a sort of school in
between the two, that accepted me. It was a rather snobbish
combination of teachers and chaperones and girls trying to
find the best way to spend time before their real lives
actually began. By life they meant marriage. By marriage, a
horsy country life, opening charity bazaars. So we were
taught how to make a speech for such occasions. They also
taught us some history and English literature; some dancing
and acting; we visited London, its museums and galleries;
we learned the kind of table manners which forbid you to
ask for sugar or milk until it is offered to you; we slept four

in each room and the girls stole everything I had. I was hungry, ate chocolates, and got fat.

The next term, after Christmas, Clara went to Austria and I transferred to the convent in Cavendish Square where she had been staying. Strangely, I loved it.

The nuns here were intelligent and understanding. I wrote in a paper one day that when I really liked a book very much, I stopped reading it and read only one page every day to keep it longer, as I felt that when I got to the end I would lose those friends that the characters in the book had become for me and that I had come to love. The "Mother" who taught us literature sent for me. "How interesting," she said, "do you really feel that way?" I think she understood. From then on I had a heavenly time writing papers for her and then discussing them with her.

They took us to the National Gallery, where we sat on stools listening to a dreary professor describe a picture for thirty minutes; but from then on I loved pictures.

In my same school there was an Italian girl whom I used to call "the tiger" because she was so terrified of everything. From nine to nine thirty in the morning we were allowed to go out for a walk; I would run, dragging "the tiger" behind me down the streets to a café where we could drink a malted milk shake and eat chocolate cake. We became fatter and fatter. I laughed madly because "the tiger" was afraid of being discovered at a milk bar, which was not allowed; afraid to be back late for school; afraid to be found out with chocolate cake in her room; afraid her mother would scold her for putting on weight. I adored "the tiger"; she was absolutely the opposite of me in every possible way.

I went to church; I prayed for hours; I became deeply religious. I felt the fascination of that semi-dark, silent chapel where you could abandon yourself to thinking.

When I came back to Italy the maids had changed. Jolanda, a young girl from Forte dei Marmi who had come to the house when she was fifteen and used to help in the kitchen, had now graduated to children's maid. She was in love with the chauffeur from Rome, who was spitefully called the "Romano." Jolanda was gay and happy and full of energy and answered back to everyone in broad Tuscan. Vigiassa had gone to the *guardaroba*. She now wore black, felt very important, and looked after the washing, ironing, and housekeeping. I missed her tearful scenes and whispered gossip.

Clara was eighteen. Boys and men flocked around. One or two of them held my hand and said they wanted to marry me. I roared with laughter.

I walked into Gianni's room one morning, he was naked and I saw he had become a man.

My mother was nervous; Lotti was around, being pestered as usual. Miss Parker was slightly put off by my jokes about the English girls. Now that I was so much taller than she was, she hugged me and said she was happy to see me.

Maria Sole had become fat and ugly. Mammà had all her hair cut off and then said she looked like a country vicar. Instead of laughing, I got mad. I told her she was being unkind and shouldn't say things like that. We quarreled.

My mother took a house in Austria for the summer and went there with Clara. I went to Forte dei Marmi with all the other children.

Princess Jane had died while I was in school. I felt responsible for the house and what went on. The maids came and asked my advice, so did the governesses. I scolded the little ones when they didn't behave and told them when it was time to go to bed. I was rather unhappy.

When Mammà came back one afternoon and, walking in the garden at sunset, told me that Clara was going to get married, I was frightfully hurt. "You mean to say Clara is going to get married and she hasn't told me?" I asked indignantly. We were friends, Clara and I; we had lived our lives together, sharing our joys and pains, laughter and sadness, and now she had completely forgotten me. I sobbed in my room that night. The next morning I could see the people in the house nudge each other saying I was jealous because Clara was getting married. How could you ever make other people understand?

*T*assilo Furstenberg was a very good-looking man: tall with a strong, thin, straight body, a wild Tartar face, a lot of uncombed hair, and extraordinarily dirty clothes.

With him the "von's" and the "zu's" and the "von und zu's," the Knights of Malta and the Hungarian princes, the Austrian countesses and the Serene Highnesses invaded our life. Lotti was so delighted she sat up day and night organizing, writing notes, sending invitations, gloating over names, mixing up everything. Signorina Corsi sat with her in the room, helping her out. She cried three times a day because someone had come into the room and not said good morning politely, treated her like a servant, not shown her enough consideration because, "Of course I, Anna Corsi, am only a bourgeois teacher and not a countess." Lotti spent half the time introducing everyone who appeared at the door to "dear Signorina Corsi, who is helping us so much; what would we ever do without her!" until she cheered up and drank three *cappuccini* all in a row and then had a terrible headache. Lotti opened the window and all was well until some new man walked passed the door, shouted, *"Ciao,* Lotti," without noticing Signorina Corsi and it started all over again.

Tassilo talked about his family with great deference and sense of humor, about both the heads of the family of the Furstenbergs and of the Festetichs, to which his mother belonged. He ground his teeth and said, "Ach, you don't understand. The head of the family is very important." He had hundreds of cousins and uncles and relatives and they were all rather shocked that he should marry a girl without a title. It would ruin his position in the Almanach de Gotha or, anyway, his children's position. His sons would not be received as Knights of Malta because you had to have so many quarters of nobility.

Nobility was still considered something very special. Thank God, we had one grandfather who was a prince, even if a rather second-rate one, or Lotti would have been too ashamed. But, because of *that* grandfather, we could corral a few Lancellottis and Massimos, who were cousins of my mother's, and would happily flock to the wedding.

My grandfather, the Senatore, also had a very weird outlook on nobility. He used. to tell us that when he was a boy his mother had sent him to the San Giuseppe Institute, where most of the boys, being nobles, were not allowed to say hello to him. He considered this totally normal and told us about it without any animosity toward the mothers of his school companions, as if relating an everyday fact. So, when he was told that Tassilo would like to be given a job at Fiat, he answered, convinced he was being very objective, "He is a prince, isn't he? Tell him to go on being a prince." And that was the end of that.

Whether this prince would wear his "Knights of Malta" red coat or his Hungarian green velvet trimmed in sables was a daily problem. Most of the Mittel Europisch nobles were extremely handsome and not very bright, but the women were even less bright, snobbish to a degree, and not even pretty. The more titles they had, the more their hands looked like a bunch of sausages.

Needless to say, I was a bridesmaid—dressed in some revolting pinkish floppy material—along with a number of young countesses dressed like me and looking down their noses at me. Gianni took Clara to the altar. The Austrian side was a shimmer of furs and colors and decorations all over their chests and around their necks, the Agnelli side dismally black.

The Turinese were enchanted with this colorful event and looked in wonder at the men dressed up as in a film.

When it was over my grandfather asked if the *carnevale* had come to an end.

Quite frankly, I never understood why Clara married Tassilo. As the years went by she explained to us, my brothers and sisters and myself, what a marvelous man Tassilo was, what a fantastic lover, what a fabulous husband; but, of course, that was rather in Clara's character. Whatever she had was always the best.

I don't think she was in love with him when they got married. She was eighteen and he twice her age. They came from totally different milieux, and they had different tastes—she liked clothes and embroidered linen, he liked to hunt in the Tirolean mountains; she liked household gossip, he liked elaborate social entertainment; she liked to lie in bed, he liked the open spaces.

They went to India and toured the maharajas for their honeymoon, then returned and stayed in my mother's house in Rome. Clara was bored stiff going out to dinner parties. She rang me and I came down from Turin and stayed with her. My mother disapproved.

Clara said, "Don't get married, it's not that amusing." I readily believed her. I had a wild adolescent crush on a cousin of Tassilo's who was beautiful, nothing else. Looking at him, one imagined the wonderful thoughts pent up in his head—they somehow never came out. But at that time what did a girl do but get married? And, if a man was considered a suitable match, everyone pushed her to do so.

Tassilo went away for a few days, so Clara took me to a party with her. I was shy and self-conscious and didn't know what to do or say. A boy came up to me. "You are a friend of my brother's," he said. I was, but the two Lanza brothers were quite different. This boy had his black hair thickly covered in brilliantine to straighten out his curls, puzzled blue-gray eyes, and attractive features that were at the same time vulgar and unusual.

"I thought you were fighting in Spain," I said.

"I was wounded," he answered, "they sent me back to get well."

At that time I did not imagine that an Italian fighting in the Spanish Civil War could be on the anti-Franco side. In the eyes of the Italian press and public, the Republicans were the rebels, while the Franco forces were the true loyalists. That fascism and antifascism were different ways of feeling—that I understood years later.

I knew that this boy was an officer of the Tercio, as Galvano, his brother, had shown me a photograph of him being decorated with a silver medal. I also knew he was brave, run after by the ladies, Sicilian, the son out-of-wed-lock of the unmarried Prince of Trabia and a married princess, which meant that he could not carry his father's title.

"Here all the women run after me, damn it, I can't stand it any longer. They are all in love with me. Please, do me a favor, don't fall in love with me."

The desperate quality of his vitality struck me. "Don't worry, Raimondo," I smiled.

He left and a cloud suddenly turned the sky to gray.

I had my seventeenth birthday in the United States —Santa Barbara, California, of all places in the world. It was April 1939. I walked up and down the beach of Santa Barbara looking at the covered, grayish, unraining sky for hours and hours and hours. The sand and the shells crunched under my feet. The ocean, as they called it, was too cold to swim in. I walked and thought. I was alone; perhaps for the first time in my life, I was alone. My Uncle Ranieri, my mother's brother, who had been married to an American sculptress, was now about to marry another American divorcée who had a twelve-year-old daughter. The bride-to-be, Lydia, had a beach house in Santa Barbara and she offered my mother, who thought I was becoming impossible, to take me with her and my Uncle Ranieri to the States. They were in love and wanted to be on their own. The daughter, Mousie, went to school and was, anyway, not exactly entertaining. So I spent most of my time alone.

Both my Uncle Ranieri and Lydia told the most fantastic lies. It was their own form of rivalry and nobody could have beaten them at it. I sat enthralled listening to how one of them had learned to speak Chinese in a week, the other had climbed a mountain barefoot on an iguana, one had raced in the Grand National on an imported Australian cart horse, the other had surfed past Hawaii on a tidal wave. Now and then I contradicted. This they would not permit; we had a row. I retired to my room, held my head between my hands, and asked myself why human beings were born. Ranieri was very handsome and charming; Lydia could be great fun. They were kind to me, and I knew I was a bore to them. I tried to be human, tolerant, understanding. At seventeen it is so difficult.

They got married in New York in the River House, where Lydia had a flat, and then we sailed back to Europe. I had seen the Grand Canyon, Long Island, Harlem, and most of America from a train window.

I am forgetting. I had also seen the World's Fair.

On the *Conte di Savoia* sailing home, I remember the businessman Marzotto saying at the dinner table, "Well, next it will be the Rome World's Fair. Shall we ever see that *'E Quaranta-due?*"

*T*opazia Caetani was having her coming-out ball at the Excelsior in Rome. I wasn't eighteen yet, but my mother decided I had better go and meet some people instead of saying I was in love with this Austrian prince and sitting in Turin teaching poor children how to do their homework in the parish church.

I wore the most décolleté dark-green-velvet dress while all the other girls wore white lace and ruffles. I arrived with six boys that my mother had invited to dinner. I was monstrously shy and knew no one. I couldn't dance and hated it.

Raimondo dragged me into an empty room and kissed me distractedly and violently on my mouth. "Didn't you tell me you had never kissed a man?" he asked.

"I hadn't."

"Well, why are you kissing me? I thought you were in love with your Austrian genius."

"I was," I answered. He squeezed my hand and left.

He was forever leaving, this Raimondo, and then appearing in the middle of the day, or the night. When he came into a room it was like lightning. Everybody stopped talking or interrupted what they were doing; he shouted, laughed, kissed everybody, joked. He ate like a garbage-shredding machine, drank like a thirsty desert garden, played the piano, telephoned, and held my hand—all at the same time. He rushed up the stairs and stood panting, he drove a car like a lunatic, he lay at the foot of my bed and talked incessantly, then, suddenly, stood up, kissed me, and disappeared.

My mother said I must come back to Turin immediately. I took the night train and stood at the window watching Rome disappear while my heart became smaller and smaller. Somebody touched my shoulder. I grew extremely irritated when I saw Youssouf, an Albanian boy who I knew fancied me, standing beside me there at the window while the Palidoro fields rushed by. He had studied in Paris and was terribly intelligent. He said he loved me, he was in love with me, he had followed me to tell me that he was mad about me. He would have given his life to be able to take me to a forest in Albania for two years and educate me. He would give me books to read, he would teach me about art and history and literature. How was it possible that I should throw away my brains and intelligence going around with silly people who had nothing to say? As puffs of smoke from the engine invaded the Wagon-Lit corridor, he said, "Please study, learn, read. Don't waste yourself like this. *Je suis tellement amoureux de toi que j'arriverais même à t'épouser,*" he added.

I listened through a steamy pillow of my own thoughts that were rocking inside my head.

The next morning when we got off the train he went to a hotel and I invited him home for lunch. When he arrived, my grandfather had already telephoned to know who the man was who had followed me from Rome and what his intentions were. I was so annoyed with Youssouf that I was rude to him. My mother kindly made me notice it; I became even ruder. After lunch he once more told me that he loved me.

"Leave me alone," I finally shouted. "Can't you see that you bore me stiff?"

He left. I was ashamed. I was in love with Raimondo, but I couldn't keep myself from thinking about what Youssouf had said. He was right; I was ignorant. I had completely stopped studying. I hung around waiting, I didn't know what for.

*O*n the autumn of 1939 Gianni and Galvano, Raimondo's brother, were doing their military service together in Pinerolo where the great cavalry regiments trained. They appeared in Turin, their heads shaved, to spend their few hours of leave, looking cold and hungry like two little lost soldiers who have their picture taken holding hands.

Now everybody was talking of war. I beseeched my

mother to use all her influence in the Red Cross so that they would let me train as a nurse at once, instead of my having to wait until I was twenty-one, which was the rule. Finally, after endless discussions, disapproving and skeptical looks from the titled ladies who ran the Red Cross voluntary nursing service in Italy, and all sorts of menacing advice, I was accepted as a student nurse and Lotti was asked to do the same and keep an eye on me.

We wore an elaborate, white, starched uniform with strange nunlike underveils and half sleeves. The maids complained that no evening dress of my mother's had ever given them so much trouble to keep in order.

They taught me that a nurse should never run, as it is not dignified, so I walked with calm possession of my limbs until I came to an empty corridor in which I would run at full speed. In no time I was being sent to do every errand in the hospital, old and enormous as it was, as I took half the time of anyone else to run through it. The smell of the people still revolted me but I learned not to be sick by thinking wildly about something I liked. The patients asked for me. I was so strong I could carry practically any woman out of bed in my arms. I was very young, while most of the other nurses were not, and I was clean. I spoke very bad Piedmontese to the women from the market place in Porta Palazzo and they roared with laughter. One doctor, with skin so black he looked like an olive, asked for my help all the time. I was forbidden to talk to him. The nuns who ran the hospital (the nurses only came in the morning) were kind only to the doctors; they were nasty to the patients, who detested them.

The wards were enormous with two long lines of beds, one on either side. When somebody was about to die they put a screen around three sides of the bed so the others wouldn't see. It was even worse. I remember one girl hugging me and panting, "Don't let me die. I don't want to die. Please, do something so I won't die." I held her in my arms, her hands around my neck, until a sister came and took me away saying, "You are crazy! That girl is very infectious, she is dying of tuberculosis. Go home now and wash." The next morning the girl had disappeared. She had died. I could hear her voice saying, "Please, don't leave me alone" with a despairing, begging wail that followed me for days.

In the afternoon I went to classes and then studied until bedtime. I was going to show them how that little Agnelli girl could do things seriously.

I got up early and went riding before it was time to go to the hospital. My grandfather had bought an enormous piece of land with a big round manège on it that used to belong to a famous Turinese businessman. The plant of the new Fiat Mirafiori would be built on that land, but until then I was allowed to go and gallop in the fields.

I fell off my horse and broke three ribs. I lay in bed and Emilio Pucci, who had just broken his leg skiing in Sestriere, came to visit. A heavy cast covered his leg, which he rested on a chair as he reclined in an armchair at the foot of my bed.

A maid came running down the corridor. "The Senator," she panted, "the Senator is here. He has come to visit you."

"Oh God, Emilio," I said anxiously, "please disappear, quick!"

He looked at me. "How?" he blurted.

The door was already open. My grandfather walked in and looked suspiciously at this man in my bedroom. He sat for a few minutes, then left and immediately rang my cousin Laura to find out who this Pucci was and whether I was going to marry him. Laura laughed. Emilio had a crush on her.

In the mornings when I arrived in my ward I was red in the cheeks and warm from riding and the other nurses looked paler and older. Some of them disliked me out of principle. Others accepted me, invited me to tea in their houses, and called me La Agnellina. I was delighted to think I had friends of my own, a life where I was a person, people who smiled because I had said good morning.

It was still the custom for girls to go in chaperoned groups on sightseeing trips so my cousin Berta, a girl friend, and myself left for Sicily, accompanied by a maid. Raimondo met us and took us around, sent us to look at ruins, swallowed ten enormous ice creams in a row at a table at Rageth e Koch, the elegant *gelateria* where the Sicilians ate ices and *granita di caffè* all day long. He showed us his grandmother's villa in the center of Palermo with a garden as big as a village. Dozens of cousins of his lived there in utter confusion, greeting each other very formally as "Principessa" or "Cousin," and kissing each other's hand or cheeks.

We went to the miserable center of the town where they fried cows' entrails at the street corners, to the fish market which had swordfish as long as the tables they were sold from, to dark churches, down sunny roads with geranium-lined walls, to the ruins of temples and the Monreale cloister, to strange villas and scented gardens, through orange groves, down beaches, up dusty steps.

Raimondo's grandmother, the Princess of Trabia, invited us for lunch. We wore silk *chemisier* dresses and stockings and shoes. She lived in the Palazzo Butera which had an enormous terrace overlooking the port. The huge *saloni* were lined in red brocade, heavy curtains kept the sunshine out, every inch of space was covered in carpets, pictures, furniture; all the plates one ate off were silver. The atmosphere was dramatic, imposing, and Oriental. You could hardly believe that outside you had the sea and the screaming, begging, dark-skinned children.

The chairs had very high backs. Raimondo sat very straight. If now and then he absent-mindedly leaned backward, his grandmother would look at him firmly, even if with a smile, and say, "R-raimōndo" in a very Sicilian accent.

"Scusami, Nonna," he answered and sat up straight again.

He explained to me later that his grandmother was afraid he would soil the chairs with the brilliantine he wore on his hair. This palace was his home since his father had died when he was a young boy. He had been brought up by his grandmother in this churchlike atmosphere that had nothing to do with reality. I remember his mother telling me that when she had arrived in Sicily with her two sons for the funeral of their father, the Princess of Trabia had looked at them and exclaimed, "This one," looking at Raimondo, "you can see is a Trabia, but why is the other one so fair?" The mother had the blondest hair you have ever seen.

So Galvano had gone back with his mother to her home near Venice, and Raimondo had stayed on in Sicily. The two brothers were great friends and adored each other, perhaps because they were so different. Raimondo teased Galvano about his laziness, his vagueness, his selfishness, his greediness, his noncaring attitude toward life in general. Galvano laughed.

The Princess of Trabia had a beautiful, rather hard, very white face. She was intelligent, shrewd, piercing. She asked why we had come to Palermo, who was accompanying us, what we had visited. We lied pretending Berta was much older than her age and that we were accompanied not by a maid but by a governess who had stayed in the hotel because of a headache. She listened, knowing we were lying, enjoying our embarrassment.

Then Raimondo drove us to Trabia where he had a castle on the coast where a waterfall ran through the terrace and leaped into the sea. Ahead, in the bay, was the *tonnara*. You could see the little flags and the big flat boat that signaled the nets for the tuna fish. We stayed there for the night. Raimondo took me out in a boat on the moonlit sea; he hoped the tuna would come into the net so that we could see the *mattanza* (the kill) when they pulled the fish out of the last net with big hooks. The sea became red with blood and Raimondo would dive into the *camera della morte* and swim up and down while the fishermen cheered.

We all sat around the radio. It was June 1940. You could hear the crowds cheering in Piazza Venezia. We had heard them four years before when Mussolini announced we were going to conquer Abyssinia or that Italy finally had an empire. It had always seemed remote and rather farcical.

Now the tension was different. It refracted from the streets and the corridors of the house, turning the room into a crystallized breath-holding moment. *"Saluto al Duce!"* shouted a voice into the microphone and then we listened to the declaration of war, against England and France, with the Germans. There were tears in my mother's eyes. Miss Parker blew her nose. For us, war was an unknown adventure, and when one is young the things you are not familiar with have a strange attraction.

Gianni was still doing his officers' training course. We had no other man in the family who could be sent to the front, so life went on more or less as usual.

Then the disaster of the French front occurred. The Italian soldiers sent to fight in the Alps returned on stretchers, their feet frozen and gangrenous, their gaze astonished and hopeless.

In my nurse's uniform every morning I bicycled up to the hospital where my mother's nursing school operated, with Lotti, hating the idea, bicycling behind me. We spent the day looking after the wounded soldiers, listening to their tales of how they had been sent walking into the snow without socks in their leaking cardboard boots, of how they had been massacred while they hardly knew what was happening to them. A ward in wartime is completely different from a normal hospital ward. Young boys looking healthy and sunburned suddenly reveal an amputated leg or a bloody wound, the stench of gaseous gangrene filling the air, the smile turning to pain and disillusionment.

The excitement, gone so soon, had left most of the Italians stunned and worried. The look on the older people's faces was tense, desperate.

We were still young and still believed that, around the corner, life was going to be full of flowering trees.

I asked if I could go into the operating theater to watch. They said I was too young, they were afraid I would faint; but the matron interceded for me and I was asked to come on a Tuesday morning.

When I walked in I saw that many of the young doctors standing around were laughing and looking at me in a strange, amused way. I stood in a corner, my white veil one inch above my eyebrows, my dress hem fifteen inches from the ground, as the uniform regulation specified.

They brought the first patient in and started draping him with white sheets. They covered his legs and chest, then his thighs and abdomen, then more and more until only the penis of the boy was left bare. They performed the operation, then brought in another boy and went through the same procedure, again and again. Now and then one of the doctors would glance at me to see how I was reacting. I don't think I ever moved. I watched in silence and pretended to be totally unaffected.

At the end one doctor turned to me and asked, "Well, Sister Agnelli, was it interesting?" and they all burst out laughing.

"Thank you very much," I said, "it was," and walked out.

I loathed their vulgar minds, their childish sexual complex, their wanting to embarrass me, their ridiculous way of asserting what they considered was their male superiority.

I learned then that men do regard their penis as a fantastic object. The soldiers who were in the surgical ward because their appendix had been removed would call to me and say, "Please, nurse, have a look at my scar. It hurts." When I came to their bedside they would reveal an astonishing erection which left me cold, as it was only later that I learned what it meant. The other nurses giggled and screamed, "Cover yourself up, you naughty boy!" I seriously observed the scar. I am afraid it became the sport of the ward.

One day a doctor came up to me and said, "Don't you believe in this world at all, Sister Agnelli? Do you really believe that only the next world exists? You always seem to be looking into the next world."

"No, no. I like this world very much," I assured him.

But evidently our worlds were different.

I was on holiday when Raimondo rang and said he would be arriving that night by train. I managed to get a taxi to go and meet him a few miles away from Forte dei Marmi at the Viareggio station.

In wartime Italy all stations were forever crowded to the point of madness so that the impression you got was half holiday, half earthquake. I stood squeezed, pushed, bustled by the hundreds of people in the dim light trying to understand from the perpetually screeching loudspeakers when Raimondo's train would arrive. Everyone shouted, tried to see who would appear, what was happening.

I wore a white-and-blue-striped dress and carried in my hand three gardenias that someone had given me as I drove off. I clutched my gardenias and stood looking fixedly at the gate through which the crowds of passengers poured.

Then I saw him; his vitality bursting out of his shirt collar, which was open with his tie dangling around it; his arrogant, sweet, inquisitive look and his surprised smile as he discovered me.

"You are mad," he said as he kissed me. "I really never thought of taking that train. It is by pure chance that I took it; it was the last thing I thought I would do."

"But you said you were coming," I murmured.

"I never do what I say."

He kissed me again. He dragged me to the taxi, he held

my hand, he turned, looked at me, and exclaimed, "What's happened to you? You have become good-looking!"

We had no car but bicycled miles away on the empty roads. We sailed, friends came and stayed endlessly, we lay for hours on our stomachs on the beach, talking about our lives in that future which seemed so short. At night we sat around the big pantry table and ate whatever we could find, talking, talking, talking, until we walked out again and watched the sun rising over the sea, sprinkling the gray, cold sand with silver dust; then we fell into bed exhausted, cold, and young.

The next day on the beach I watched Raimondo walking near the fringe of the waves. His round buttocks, his creamy skin, his wide, sensuous shoulders triggered a shivering sensation in the bottom of my belly. It was the first time I experienced sexual attraction and realized it was something independent, different, far away from love. But then, I was in love with Raimondo already and the sensation gave me a feeling of loss and happiness and despair all mixed up together. He did not leave as he always did after two days. He held my hand and talked to me forever. He lay by my side and I knew the sweetness of his skin against mine, the bliss of thinking in two, of living a world of your own, of not knowing if you are asleep or awake, if it is morning or evening, if there is a war, if the sun is shining, of not knowing anything except that you are together.

*R*aimondo was a great friend of Galeazzo Ciano. Galeazzo would dine with him in Rome and take him along on official trips to make everybody laugh with his imitations of the German Ambassador or the Fascist *gerarchi.* He was allowed everything.

Ciano was the social image of power. He played golf and the whole of Roman society took up golf. They gathered at the golf club for lunch waiting like beggars for Galeazzo's *ciao.* The women behaved with a lack of dignity that was embarrassing. Galeazzo's *favorita* of the moment was adulated, envied, loathed, run after. To hold on to Galeazzo's arm for a moment in public and to be pawed by him was the sign of success. God knows, although we later became good friends and I was very fond of him, Galeazzo was not an attractive man. His chin sticking out over his second chin and his fat stomach, his slick hair, the small beady eyes with a yellowish glow, the rather short arms and legs were of a piece with the shrill, nasal, high-pitched voice with which he arrogantly addressed the people around him. Whatever he said, they all doubled up in laughter. I think he hated them all.

One evening Raimondo brought Galeazzo home to one of our pantry parties. My friends, the boys I talked with all night, disappeared in discreet disapproval.

"What are you going to offer us?" Galeazzo asked in his falsetto shout.

"I don't know, some biscuits, I suppose, and perhaps some chocolates; and there might be some wine to drink."

The ladies of the "court" following him started to twitter nervously. "But you must have something else."

"No," I said. There wasn't. My mother disapproved of buying things on the black market and even the chocolates were a rare exception.

We sat, the ladies, ambassadors, ministers, minstrels who followed Galeazzo, waiting for his reaction. He laughed, they laughed.

Galeazzo was worried because he was going back to

Rome to have his tonsils out and everyone assured him that it wasn't in the least painful. I was silent.

He turned to me and asked, "Aren't you a nurse? What do you think, is it going to hurt?"

"Very much," I answered and there was an uproar.

The women threw their arms up in the air, the men shook their heads, "Really, Suni! How can you say something so monstrous? You know it's not going to hurt Galeazzo at all, so why make him nervous?"

I was silent again. I looked for Raimondo's hand and held it.

Leaving, Galeazzo said, "I am not allowed to say *'lei'* by the regime, so we are going to say *'tu'* to each other."

I answered very politely using the *lei*.

The women went away delighted. Certainly this was not a house from which to fear competition.

"Isn't he terrible?" I said to Raimondo. "And yet, I rather like him. He is clever, if only he didn't have those terrible people around him."

The doors on the corridor opened one by one and my friends reappeared. We sat around the pantry table. We tried to laugh; it was not the same as the other nights. I knew they felt betrayed.

Raimondo went to Rome for a few days. He then rang to say that he would meet me near Livorno where Galeazzo, who was going to some fishing event, had invited us, and would send a car for me. For some reason I got there very late and Raimondo had gone off on a fishing boat with the others, so they rowed me out through the nets and the swarming fish. As we came nearer, I could see him on the deck in his light suit standing between the others who were all dressed in dark ones. I was shy, and afraid of what would happen when I saw Raimondo again. All those men whom I hardly knew around him made me nervous.

They asked me to stay in the rowboat and help lift the fish out of the net. There were so many fish; fat, alive, jumping, cold, slippery, wet, moon-colored, shining, that in a moment the boat was full. We went back to the pier and at last I was able to get near to Raimondo. For once he wasn't laughing. He caught my hand and held it in silence. He was suffering and I couldn't understand what had happened to him.

Later, when we were alone, he said, "I always told you I liked freedom more than anything. I don't care about freedom; I want to marry you. I love you."

Galeazzo took us back to his house in Antignano and sat me next to him for dinner with Raimondo on my other side. Galeazzo laughed and said, "You tell the truth. The operation was terrible, my throat hurt like hell. You were the only honest person who told me it would. I wanted to send you a telegram."

We became friends. He did not bring his lady friends to his house, where the children he adored were with him. There were ministers, advisers, Fascist *gerarchi*, friends from the town, but it was a family atmosphere—even if one did drink champagne at all meals.

After dinner, Raimondo took me into the garden and made a scene. "You never talked to me all through dinner! You talked to Galeazzo all the time. I'll beat you, I'll show you!"

I was totally stunned. "You are joking," I said. "What do you expect me to do, turn my back on my host and talk to you all the time? Why do you bring me here if you want me to be rude? You seem to think I am one of those bitches who can't talk to a man without flirting with him. Anyway, let's get out of here. Let's go back home, I've had enough."

We went back to Forte dei Marmi. It was September. The sea was bluer, the air cooler, we never slept, we lay in the sailboat looking at the wind, we listened to "Ohi Mari, Ohi Mari" over and over again. We talked, we laughed, we held hands.

"What are you going to do if one day you need both hands?" people asked us.

Happiness is so short you can really get along with only one hand while it lasts.

I lay in bed with pleurisy. Raimondo's grandmother came to visit me.

My mother was wearing a two-piece bathing suit, which was very unusual at the time, so I asked her to put on something more appropriate for the occasion. As the Princess of Trabia walked black and slowly into the room, Mammà appeared in a charming, *comme il faut* dress.

Raimondo stood up. His grandmother looked piercingly at the room, the big double bed in which I was lying, me, her grandson. She sat in an armchair. "Don't take aspirin, child," said the Princess of Trabia. "They killed my son with aspirin."

I was paralyzed with embarrassment. The Princess of Trabia talked very little. When she left she again said, "Remember, don't take aspirin."

They sent me to a sanatorium in Davos.

White rooms, gray-white corridors, white nurses, the Grand Duke Dimitri in one room and a nymphomaniac German lady in another, a Portuguese boy, a Swiss lute player, old men, old women, quiet.

To reach the Schatzalp Sanatorium you had to take a funicular. It only ran at certain hours, very rarely in the off-season. *The* season was winter when the children brought their bobsleds and slid down the ice track. But when we arrived it was autumn and the short walk from the funicular station to the entrance of the sanatorium was brown, dull, cold.

The cure consisted of lying in bed, on the balcony or inside the room with the windows open, and breathing in the air that was supposed to make you healthy. As everyone was in bed practically all the time and the windows were open, there wasn't much point in heating the place, so they didn't.

Poor, dear, sweet Lotti, who had accompanied me and who wasn't sick, sat around the place in coats, plaids, woolen stockings, fur-lined boots, still shivering.

The daytime was fascinating. Lying in total silence in a bed full of hot-water bottles and blankets, watching the snowflakes falling or the distant white mountain flecked with black pine trees is something very similar, as a sensation, to lying in the sun in the middle of the sea after a swim in cold water. One drifts away, floats, feels, and doesn't think. One knows through the skin that one is alive.

But at dusk, when they brought you back into your room at five o'clock and gave you hot chocolate to drink with zwiebacks to dip into it and there you were in that polished aquarium-like box with nothing to do but wait until tomorrow, that was agony. Lotti sat on a chair doing nothing, and we waited for the moment when we could go to sleep.

I wrote Raimondo letters. I missed him; there wasn't

much to say. I felt that in some way I had let him down. I knew I wasn't sick. I was tired, but I didn't know what I was tired of.

I got a strange skin disease which itched like hell. I tried to explain to the doctors that I might have scabies as Raimondo had picked it up on some train but had got rid of it in three days. They smiled with spiteful superiority, "Scabies is a soldier's disease. This is nothing that simple." They called in specialists from all over the place. My mother decided I had some strange venereal disease. They covered me with ointments and brushed me with medicines. I itched more and more.

Raimondo announced his arrival. I was allowed to go to the station and meet him. I stood in the dismal Davos Platz station watching the train come in through the snow. The Swiss station chime went "dang-dang," the stationmaster shouted "Davoooos Plaaatz," a few passengers stepped off the train, and Raimondo wasn't there. I took the funicular back, lay on my bed, and cried.

Later in the evening Raimondo rang. He had mixed up the train timetables, was trying to get them to run a special funicular. He mentioned he had brought me a present.

I waited for him as the funicular crept slowly up the mountain. He wore a blue scarf around his neck, looked cold and pale, and had, on a leash, the most enormous white and black harlequin great Dane that ever lived. He was as big as a horse, beautiful, quiet, strong, and majestic. While nobody looked we took him into the sanatorium and upstairs. When he moved the room shook. He drank a bathtub of water. His name was Nador.

I lay in bed with my arms around Raimondo and knew that things were never going to be the same. Raimondo was made for madness, open spaces, freedom. He really wasn't

made for ordinary life. I was sad because I loved him and
could feel what he felt. I was sorry for him and there was
nothing I could do about it.

Anyway, the uproar produced by the discovery of Nador
in my bedroom the next morning was enough to make us
laugh for three days.

O n Cortina, where they had allowed me to go a few
months later, I began to feel better.

Raimondo and I became engaged. My mother came
back from Rome one day bringing a beautiful engagement
ring and bracelet that had been given to her for me by
Raimondo's grandmother. Now and then I would put the
ring on my finger and look at it. It had nothing to do with
Raimondo or me.

I was afraid of getting sick again. I took my temperature
every two minutes. I went to a local doctor and asked him
what he thought was the matter with my skin.

"You've got scabies, of course," he said and laughed.
"Put this on and you'll be all right in three days."

It was the vilest smelling thing you could think of but it
cured me.

Every day I spoke to Raimondo on the telephone. We
were supposed to get married in June but we didn't talk
about it often. He told me of the people he went out with,
the women he went to bed with, how different they all were
from me whom he loved. I wasn't jealous—not then.
Between us there was something different.

I wrote him long letters and he told me about how he
would sit in his bathtub and read them. He lived in a suite

in the Grand Hotel that was full of records, cigarettes, brown velvet, photographs, and newspapers. When he wasn't in a very big bed with some woman he was generally talking on the telephone. But he was still always rushing and always late.

Back in Rome I waited for him for hours in the Piazza Colonna, where he would pick me up to take me to lunch in some *trattoria*. I once mentioned I had waited for an hour and forty minutes.

"Now, Nini, please!" he exclaimed. "You weren't really expecting me to be punctual."

He was right. I laughed.

He would sit at the table, put an enormous pile of newspapers on it, then read them all, one after the other. In the meantime he would hold my hand and, now and then, lift his head and say, "Do you love me, Nini?"

I did.

"Thank God you are not one of those boring women who say, 'You prefer the newspaper to me' and sulk. I love you."

I was happy with him when he was his selfish self and didn't feel obligated or tied down. I was very young.

I was in Turin when Raimondo began telling me that he was going out with a young actress, at the time rather successful, whom he was very attracted to physically. I was surprised to hear that this girl was suddenly invited to the houses of the most exclusive princes where usually no one was chic enough to be asked. But I knew that if Galeazzo mentioned that he wanted somebody to be invited with him, all doors were open; and this was evidently the case. Raimondo got more and more involved. Roman society wagged its tongue over such gossip, so one day I took the train and went to Rome.

Galeazzo asked me to go and see him in his office at the
Palazzo Chigi and I walked into the marble waiting room
with great curiosity. It was full of busy ushers and standing
people who immediately led me with understanding smiles
to a small sitting room with a purple-velvet-covered sofa.

Galeazzo came in, sat down next to me, and put his arm
around my shoulder. I was rather embarrassed. He told me
that Raimondo had quite lost his head over this girl and
that I had better forget him.

Then Galeazzo asked me, "Forgive my being indiscreet,
but were you Raimondo's mistress? I mean, did he make
love to you?"

I was horrified, even though I knew that he was trying to
be kind. "Raimondo is Sicilian," I answered, "he wants to
marry a virgin."

"Ahh," he breathed with relief, "then it's not so bad.
Raimondo is a gentleman. I take my hat off to him."

I left, walked across the Piazza to a café, went to the
bathroom and vomited.

Feelings didn't matter. It was virginity that mattered and
Roman society could feel noble again.

Raimondo said yes, it was true, he was mad about the girl.
But what does it matter? It is the person you love which
counts, not the one you want to go to bed with. That you
get· over.

"Wait," he said, "please wait. I'll get over this in a month
or two and then we'll get married."

I left. I went back home. I put my case so brilliantly to
the duchess who was head of the Turin Red Cross nurses
that, in spite of my age, ten days later I went to Naples and
embarked on a hospital ship that carried the wounded out
of Africa.

Part Three

The Italian hospital ships were beautiful boats: well equipped, well kept, well organized. Everything that had to do with the Navy was of superior quality to the rest of the Italian outfits. When a nurse boarded a ship, she was entitled to the whistle salute reserved for officers.

I walked up the gangplank, excited, desperate, proud. The nurses had a suite of six cabins reserved for them, two by two. All the other nurses of the group were Milanese, middle aged or over thirty at least, and very suspicious of my presence. I heard one of them say, "Oh God, this war! And now we have the little Agnelli with a broken heart, too."

For supper we changed into our white uniforms and veils, ironed and starched to perfection. We sat at a separate table, and when supper was finished we stood in a row in front of the table and answered politely to the officers who chose to talk to us. There were Navy officers and doctors, a priest, press correspondents. Everything was extremely formal and respectable. After ten minutes, we left and retired to our quarters.

The head of the Italian Red Cross by tradition was a Princess of the House of Savoy, and its *Ispettrici* all over Italy belonged to the most noble families. These ladies were in constant torment that nurses might not be taken seriously, or be considered "fast." On the ships their greatest worry was to keep the *sorelle* away from any male company so that they would live up to the romantic image of womanhood, Madonna, mother, idealized sister, which all Italians adored. To accomplish this, Red Cross Headquarters tended to embark old, possibly ugly, very Catholic nurses, even if they were in fact poorly trained. It was better to be a middle-aged countess than a brilliant surgical aide.

My group, that first one I was shipped with, happened to be, by sheer chance, led by an extremely intelligent, adorable woman who was studying Oriental languages at Naples University. She had been promoted on the spot when the original *capo gruppo* left and that was why they had a vacancy into which I had been pushed.

We became great friends, Tina and I. I doted on her. She had a fabulous sense of humor and judged people with a clear, relentless, penetrating eye mitigated by extreme charity. She had a quiet, melodious voice. We talked for hours. I liked to imitate people. She saw the amusing side of the silly pompous doctors and together we laughed.

She decided that I would be in charge of the officers' department under her supervision. The other nurses were annoyed. It was the custom that the oldest nurse of the group would look after the officers, so as to keep them away from any temptation. Friends of mine who had sailed home on hospital ships had told me of seventy-year-old little deaf nurses running around giving camomile tea to the wounded men.

Tina shrugged her shoulders. "She can speak several languages. We are going to embark many prisoners, I need her there."

To me she said, "I need a person who doesn't think every officer is a Casanova."

The director and the doctors were surprised but they agreed.

We sailed to Africa: Bengasi, Tobruk, Mersa Matrûh. It took us three days to get there. We made the beds and prepared the material in the wards. We washed and ironed our uniforms in preparation for the return trip. I learned to iron, to sew on buttons, to stick the red cross on my uniforms and aprons with sweet white gum. At sunset I sat on deck and looked at the sea. I prayed. I thought about Raimondo and tears came to my eyes.

We had agreed that I wouldn't write to him for two months and that at the end of this time we would talk about future plans. He had given me his ring, an old *chevalière* that turned into a key, which he always wore, and I wore it on a chain around my neck. At night before I went to sleep I put it in my mouth and sucked it.

I was so excited that when the African beach was still far away I was already standing on the deck. The wind from the desert, wild and hot, had just begun to stroke the ship.

As we approached the shore, large rafts came toward us. The wounded men lay on stretchers, their bloody bandages red in the strong sun, their skin sunburned, the sea like enamel. Those who could not walk were carried aboard in nets that were lowered to the rafts. Then the stretchers were all lined up on the hot, windy deck so that the doctors could assign the men to the right ward: officers, noncommissioned officers, soldiers; the critical, wounded, sick. You could recognize the Italians by the color of their skin; the Germans were blond and proud, some had their red, white, and black ribboned medals pinned onto their bandaged chests; the English laughed, their flesh creamy and vulnerable; some of the prisoners were black.

One boy, very young, with a lost, adolescent, trembling voice tugged at my skirt. *"Madame, je suis un officier."* He repeated, *"Je suis français et je suis officier."*

I pointed him out to the doctor. "If he is French he is only a traitor," was the answer I got.

The deck was a confusion of stretchers, shouts, orders, wails. We went around giving the men glasses of lemonade. It was stifling hot and it took a long time to get all the wounded to their berths.

This was the first direct look I had of the front line: flesh torn up, despair, pain, missing limbs, young eyes questioning, utter nonsense, medals, pride, adventure.

*T*he next morning when I rushed down to the ward I found a roomful of British officers making fun of a small Italian attendant who, totally unaware of what was going on, kept up a conversation which he evidently thought brilliant. *"Questo Mersa Matrûh,"* he pointed out of the window.

"Oh, is it? Why, I can't believe it," roared the officers who had just left the place.

"Noi vincere guerra," the attendant went on.

"Well, I wouldn't be so sure, young chap, not with soldiers like you around."

I broke the meeting up and asked the attendant to leave. He said he was standing guard on the prisoners. I asked him to stay outside the door. I spoke to the officers and told them to, please, get back into bed.

"Where did you learn your English?" they exclaimed.

"From my governess," I answered. They went back to bed.

Some of them had shaved heads. They told me that after their capture the commander of the Italian camp had done this to spite them. I was ashamed. It is hard to be on the side of people you are ashamed of, so I tried to fight the feeling off.

A doctor came in and asked me to interpret for him.

"Where are you wounded?"

"Sister, do you know England?"

"Please, answer the doctor's question."

"How come you are so tall, Sister?"

The doctor became nervous.

"Please," I begged, "please. You are going to get me into trouble."

Then they behaved. In the afternoon they asked me if it was true that I was Miss Fiat and wanted to know what I thought of the war.

The German officers made a row and said that unless the noncommissioned officers and the soldiers got the same food as they were given in this ward they would go on a hunger strike. The Italians answered that it was regulations. Finally the Germans calmed down.

At Naples they delayed the carrying ashore of the wounded because the Princess of Piedmont was coming aboard to greet them. She arrived in her Red Cross uniform surrounded by other aristocratic nurses and proceeded to distribute sweets and oranges to the astonished men. I stood at the end of the English officers' ward. I curtsied. Somebody murmured to her who I was. She looked at me for a moment, then said, "How tall she is."

She was terribly shy and managed to speak German to the Italians, Italian to the English, and English, to their horror, to the Germans.

That evening Tina and I sat and wondered about what would happen to our country.

$\mathcal{T}$he mail came. It was an exciting moment.

Tina held all the letters in her hand and distributed them. Now and then she would look at me, smile, and put a letter at the bottom of the heap. I fidgeted, jumping from one foot to the other. When she had finished dealing out all the letters she still held a few in her hand.

"These are for you, Leoncino," she would say, "but you must learn to be patient. I'll give them to you later."

I sighed. I had already received by messenger a big white envelope with "The Minister of Foreign Affairs" engraved on its back. Galeazzo hoped I was all right and that I was not having too hard a time. He was kind and thoughtful, even if his letters did not make me popular on the ship.

Finally Tina pulled out the letters and I plunged into my family's and friends' news, keeping Raimondo's for last. He wrote sweetly, saying nothing, trying to be gay. I tried not to think about what would happen at the end of the two months. I did not write to him as we had agreed. To make up for it I wrote hundreds of letters and a diary that I read aloud to the other nurses. I wrote to Galeazzo and told him how awful war was when you saw it as I had seen it, and how lucky he was to have only small children. He told me later that he thought about it often.

The port of Naples was full of battleships, sailors, soldiers. We would dock alongside some other hospital ship and the nurses would pay each other formal visits. Edda Ciano was on one of them. She had had a terrible row with the Red Cross because they would not consider her a nurse until she had finished her two-year training and taken her exams. Before she had done so, they refused her application to serve on a hospital ship. She got very mad, put on a white uniform without a red cross, as she was not entitled to it, and got her father to make the Navy embark her in a cabin to herself that had nothing to do with the nurses' group. Then she acted as a nurse; everybody was happy, they all had their own way, and nobody lost face.

When we went ashore we were supposed to walk in pairs, not go into a café or public place, and practically behave like nuns. I was immediately spotted walking down the street talking to an officer and duly reprimanded.

We sailed again. It was a secret mission. We went around in the Mediterranean searching for the survivors of a torpedoed ship and never found them. We went on to Africa.

While we were sailing along, the watch spotted a yellow

speck in the distance. We came nearer and a launch was lowered. We all leaned over the railings. Three boys were lying, holding onto one another across the middle, on a semi-inflated rubber boat of the kind they carried on aircraft. They were exhausted, their delicate white skin burnt. The officer in the launch signaled to the captain on the ship: they were enemies; one boy was dead, the other two were alive. They were all half-submerged; they were carrying the dead boy like a baby.

"Leave the dead one," signaled back the captain, "bring back the other two."

The officer paused incredulous for a moment, then waited unbelieving for the order to be repeated. When the ship's chaplain understood what was going on he ran up to the captain shouting, menacing. The captain repeated the order. The dead boy was lifted overboard and his bobbing head, kept afloat by his life jacket, was dragged slowly away by the current as his friends watched speechless.

Silence fell on the ship. The chaplain gave his blessing from where he was standing at the railing, toward the sea, tears falling down his face. From then on he refused to talk to the captain. Most of us did the same.

It was midsummer. We went back and forth between Africa and Naples. I had made friends with most of the nurses, had learned to iron beautifully and served Mass for the bearded chaplain with whom I had long talks.

I had learned to bear the sight of a young soldier with a wound on the left side of his chest where you could see his heart palpitating like a sleeping sparrow, or of another, looking at his amputated stump, groaning, "What will my wife say?" My eyes were filled with horrors and suffering.

I had also met some arrogant Fascist war fans who spoke of heroism and victory, but they were very few.

They would ask me if I had a fiancé.

"Yes."

"Where is he?"

"In Rome."

"In Rome?" they were surprised. "You are engaged to a shirker? How unexpected."

It would have been difficult to try to explain. It was also difficult to understand what really was in Raimondo's mind. What was Raimondo thinking about? Life had aged me in those two months to and fro over the sea on that ship which I will not name.

One afternoon, in Naples, my mother came aboard. She wore a pale blue chiffon blouse and the ship's officers were charmed by her. She had an order from the Red Cross to have me disembarked immediately. The nurse who was going to take my place was already there.

I protested but it was useless. I obeyed and, furious, packed my suitcases. The nurses gathered around to say good-by. They asked me if they could copy my diary. I gave it to them. I had become fond of them. They were sad to see me go.

Tina put her hand on my curly hair that did look like a lion's mane and said, "Good-by, Leoncino. This Raimondo of yours, he must be a fool."

We walked off the ship, my mother and I, and the whistle blew a salute.

I looked at the little waves playing on the shore at Forte dei Marmi. The beach was emptier and bigger; I felt alone and useless. That all had ended between Raimondo and me I had understood when I had met the Princess of

Trabia walking down the steps of the Excelsior Hotel in Naples. She had stopped, looked at me sadly, half bowing in agonizing silence, as my mother dragged me away and told the chauffeur to drive to the station.

Galvano had been wounded in Africa. My mother had explained, and I had listened in stubborn silence, that Galvano was in the military hospital in Naples and that she did not want me where I would see Raimondo all the time. Raimondo was going everywhere with this girl and my mother had decided to stop this ridiculous situation.

I had been to see Raimondo in his room at the Grand Hotel in Rome. The walls were covered in photographs of the girl. He had told me he was still involved with her but he would get over it: please, would I wait. This time I had said no.

"Don't be silly, Sparrow," he explained. "Why two months, yes; four months, no? Isn't it the same thing? You know I love you; you know I want to marry you. You are too intelligent not to understand. You can't be jealous of something that has nothing to do with us."

"Why the hell do you call me 'Sparrow'?" I asked. He said it was a pretty name.

I got up and walked around the room. On one photograph was written: "To Raimondo from his Sparrow."

"No, Raimondo," I said, "no. We're not engaged any more. Good-by. And, by the way, I *am* jealous."

When Galvano's wounded leg got better, he came to Forte dei Marmi to convalesce. Raimondo arrived, we went bicycling in the *pineta*. He behaved as if nothing had changed. He said, "How marvelous that we are not engaged any more, so we can get married when we feel like it."

I didn't even bother to answer. I loved him; I was sad. I wanted to forget about the future.

Gianni had returned from the Russian front and was

about to leave for Africa. He had become a grown-up man, handsome and cynical. We never talked about the war. He would say to me, "Why do you talk about being in love? Only maids are in love. Only maids and Galvano and you. It is something for cheap magazines."

Clara was in Switzerland; my mother was worried. She was constantly taking some uncomfortable train to go visit here and there and gather advice about what to do with her children when summer ended. The war had changed course. Towns were being bombed, news from the front was bad. Life had become more difficult.

*T*he hospital ship I had just left had been torpedoed in mid-Mediterranean, announced the war bulletin that everyone was supposed to listen to standing up. She had not sunk; everyone was safe, but I could not help feeling a coward. To lie in the sun and laugh after I had seen what was going on had become impossible.

The ship on which Edda Ciano had embarked was torpedoed and sunk in the middle of the night. Three of the nurses were killed. Edda was rescued by a fishing boat as she swam away from the wreck. I went to Turin and asked to be embarked again. I saw my grandfather. He was loving and stern.

"If I were young, I'd be in love with you," he said, putting his hands proudly on my shoulders. "But I don't want you going around on those ships. You must understand: it isn't because it is dangerous, it's because I don't want my granddaughter being picked out of the sea in her nightdress by strange men."

My cousin Berta was going to marry an industrialist, Milanese and rich. Everyone said it was a marvelous match. She was happy. When she was with him she felt protected and thought about nothing.

Our friends were scattered. Lodovico, our only childhood friend, was reported missing in Russia; Emilio Pucci had become a great Air Force hero and, to everyone's astonishment, his name came up again and again in the war bulletin. Then there were the dead. Their names struck you every time. Brothers and husbands and sons of people you knew and, when you saw them, you were hopeless and at a loss for words. Boys you had played with on the beach, been to school with, danced with, talked to, had disappeared forever, far away.

Summer ended. They embarked me on another ship. We went to Yugoslavia, Albania, Greece, and carried home wounded, worn-out, sick soldiers with no light in their eyes, nothing to look forward to.

When the ship went to dry dock they sent me to the hospital at Caserta, where all the prisoners were taken care of. It was an enormous hospital whose long, high corridors were crammed with beds. We went in early to make the beds while most of the boys were still asleep. I put my hand on one's shoulder and shook him gently.

"Wake up," I said in English. "We are going to make your bed."

He was startled, looked at me with feverish eyes, and clung to my arm. "Who are you?" he shouted. "Where am I? Oh God, I thought I was at home."

I was astonished. I spent the rest of the morning doing my work and talking to the boys, who seemed delighted that I did so. I met some of the soldiers and officers who had been on my ship. They recognized me and it was like meeting old friends. A British colonel was in charge of the hospital. He was a surgeon who had been captured and he had other prisoner-doctors to help him.

After lunch I was called by the *capo gruppo*. "You are strictly forbidden to talk to the patients. These are prisoners and orders are that fraternization is not to be allowed."

"I am forbidden *what?*" I exclaimed, incredulous.

"To talk to the prisoners," she answered, livid.

"I won't stay here," I said. "I'm leaving. I refuse to look after sick people whom I'm not supposed to talk to. It is monstrous. Do you mean to say that all you nurses here, you never talk to those boys in the wards? You must be mad. I'm not going to stay here one more day."

"You forget that you belong to the Italian armed forces," she hissed. "Your orders are to stay here. You will not leave."

I left. Crammed into a packed train that took all night to reach Rome, no lights behind the blue-painted windows, standing in a corridor full of exhausted, despairing soldiers.

They sent me to another hospital ship.

*T*owns were being bombed. Our house in Turin was badly hit and burned. The little ones stayed on in Forte dei Marmi; Miss Parker had been relegated by the authorities to a room in Perugia. Galeazzo got me permission to visit her. She was lonely, sad, cold, but not complaining. Later, she was repatriated to England on a civilian train.

Italy was now full of refugees who left their bombed houses in the northern cities and tried to live in the country or in smaller towns where no military objective would attract raids. Rome was, as always, privileged; but food got scarcer and the black market boomed.

I came and went from Rome to the ships. We never knew what would happen next and invented little hiding places where we could leave messages for one another in case anything drastic happened and we would be separated by war events.

Raimondo would take me to the station every time I left, give me his ring to wear as a *porte bonheur,* and kiss me wildly on the station platform to the horror of my *capo gruppo* who said this was all right on the screen but not for a nurse in uniform.

The first time they raided the port of Naples while we were docked and dropped bombs on the ships aside ours, I felt the terror of being in a mouse trap. We sat in the center of the ship; the thud of the bombs hitting steel was worse than the explosion and shaking which followed, a dull ominous thump against which you could do nothing but go on sitting, waiting.

By now the rumor was strong that our hospital ships carried gas to Africa. The water line was lower when we left than when we returned with the ship full of wounded. One nurse telephoned Red Cross Headquarters and said they were loading her ship with gas. She was told to shut up; so we pretended we didn't know and hoped for the best.

We were approaching Tripoli one morning when a frightening explosion rocked and shook the ship and sent us running to the deck. We put on our life jackets and stood looking at the broken glass and falling plaster not knowing what had happened. We had struck a mine. From Tripoli they had seen the white ship hop into the air and then come to a standstill. The town was about to fall into enemy hands. The wounded in the hospital were waiting for the ship as their last hope to get back to Italy.

They tugged us in. The port was in utter confusion—ships, soldiers, Africans, cars, engines, bandaged men—everyone shouting, pushing, screaming. I walked up and down the docks and suddenly saw an open military car coming toward me with somebody waving. It was my brother Gianni. He had a bandaged elbow; a bullet fired accidentally by his orderly had gone through it but had done very little damage. I was so surprised I hardly reacted. He came aboard. They offered to take him back to Italy; after all, he was wounded. He smiled and refused.

They gave me leave to go away with him for the day. We drove to the ruins of Sabrata. We sat, the two of us in uniform, on the broken columns in the silent desert with the war so very near. We ate some sticky dates. Then he drove off to Tunisia.

In time we sailed back to Italy, the ship almost empty. The soldiers we had left behind watched with envious, begging eyes.

*T*he nurses became more and more nervous and shaken. On our return trip from Tripoli I sat one whole night trying to comfort a poor, rather neurotic girl whose previous ship had recently been torpedoed and sunk. The sea was rough and she was convinced that this ship, too, which had struck a mine, was suddenly going to split in half and we would be thrown into the waves. In Tripoli we had spent the nights in the hospital, but even there the bombing was practically incessant.

We were made to sit in some silly, unprotecting shelter where the flashes, the brightness from the parachuted flares with which the Allies lit the sky, the whistling sound followed by the crash of the bombs striking was all around us.

I would leave to go and watch the reflection of the fire on the sand of the desert. They told me I was crazy but, honestly, I wouldn't have minded if I died.

When I came back home that time I told my mother I thought I needed a rest. She agreed. My little brothers were in Switzerland and she suggested I join them and go skiing at Saint Moritz. It sounded rather like an anticlimax but it was exactly what I needed. One had to obtain a special authorization to be able to draw foreign currency to leave Italy. My mother arranged an appointment for me with the minister involved.

I walked in one afternoon; it was a small office and he was a small man with intelligent, tired eyes like a dying fire. I asked him for some Swiss francs so that I could go skiing for three weeks. He was surprised and faintly amused.

"Why?" he asked.

I said I was a nurse serving on hospital ships and that my last ship had hit a mine.

He interrupted me, "How old are you?"

"Twenty."

He smiled for a fraction of an instant and became stern again. "You can have the money," he said, "have a good rest."

So I went to Saint Moritz and lived in an apartment off the Palace Hotel with Giorgio and Umberto. Umberto was six or seven years old. He would get up early in the morning, put his clothes on, walk to the baker's up the snowy street, and return with lovely fresh buns for our breakfast. The delight of breakfast with Nescafé and cream and white buns and butter and jam was indescribable. When one has food all the time one totally forgets how good it can be.

Afterward I would go skiing with Topazia Caetani, who

was staying in Saint Moritz with her mother. We became great friends. At that time Topazia's attitude toward life sprang from the belief that if you were born a prince you instinctively did the right thing; if you were a bourgeois you might do the right thing if you were intelligent and thought about it long enough.

Her mother disliked me intensely because I was a bourgeois and because she was strangely envious of my mother. She would walk into Topazia's room with her face covered in some incredible beauty mask, find me sitting at the foot of Topazia's bed chatting and scream, "This room stinks."

Topazia would open the window. "It still stinks," she howled when she returned two minutes later.

"All right, Topazia, I've understood. I'm leaving. See you this evening," and I would leave laughing while Topazia signaled desperately that her mother was mad.

Topazia and I went up the double-seated ski lifts chattering. We would ski down, then resume the conversation on the next lift at exactly the point where we had left it.

"Who do you wish would fall in love with you?" she would ask as we were pushed up the steep mountain.

"A boy I met in Rome. You've never seen him. I would like him to be in love with me and I not at all with him."

"But why?"

"I think it might be fun for a change." Then we skied down.

"Would you like to be Tana Alba?" I asked on the next lift. She was in the hotel with us; very young, spoiled, her face covered in make-up and, to me, very endearing.

"I would prefer to be Babù Boncompagni. She is perfect. She has everything."

Babù was Topazia's best friend and I was faintly envious. We skied down again.

At night they all went dancing and I went back to the flat. I played with my brothers and read and thought about my future. It struck me that I had been very silly to interrupt my studies; that I wanted more than anything else to become a doctor; and that I had to find a way in which my life would depend only on myself, in which another person could never be in the position of making me go through heaven or hell. I gazed at the ceiling and saw myself walking into a ward in a white doctor's coat and the patients asking me not to leave.

I left Saint Moritz, the snow, the chocolates, the creamy cakes of soap, the peace, with my head full of how different everything was going to be.

*A*t that time in Italy it was the law that unless you had attended school regularly or taken your exams privately every year you were not allowed to take your final examination, the *maturità*, until you were twenty-three years old. I would be twenty-one in April and could not bear the idea of waiting another two years.

I started pestering my mother. We must find a way that would allow me to take that exam this year. My mother, always an angel and more so when it had something to do with keeping me away from Raimondo, went to work at once.

Galeazzo had fallen into disgrace and was no longer the Foreign Minister but the Ambassador to the Holy See. I went to see him in the Palace on the Via Flaminia. He was worried, nervous, and plotting like everybody else. I told him of my plan; he listened, concerned.

"How many years of study are you going to make up for?" he asked, slightly skeptical.

"Four or five," I murmured, slightly embarrassed.

"And you want to take the exam in three months' time?"

"Yes."

"Well, good luck. Let's see what we can do."

Somebody suggested (I forget who) that three ministers in charge promote a new law by which students who had been at the front for at least three months would be allowed to take the *maturità* exam at the age of twenty-one.

I went to see the Minister of Education with my mother. He was amused with the idea and said he would propose the law. He also suggested the best professors who could teach me Latin and Greek and the other subjects at top speed.

Cini, who was a friend of my mother's and whose daughters I knew well, was Minister of Transport. I went and spoke to him in the Hotel Excelsior while he was rushing from one meeting to another. I explained; he agreed to help.

My mother found a third minister who was willing to promote the law, and it was passed.

I bought a bicycle and a satchel that I strapped across my shoulders like the Swiss schoolchildren. My teachers all lived on the opposite side of Rome; the Gianicolo is very far from Piazza Bologna.

Between lessons I sat in public gardens doing my homework while I sucked vitamin candy that I had brought with me from Saint Moritz. I listened intently while little bearded professors in dark rooms and bosomy ladies in modern tile-floored flats taught me everything I should have learned in all those years. They all thought I was mad and couldn't possibly succeed, but they were willing to try.

I would come home pushing my bicycle up the last steep

street to our house with my head spinning with names, heroes of Greek tragedy, Latin verse, philosophical theories, laws of physics, chemistry formulas. I went to my room with the windows overlooking Rome and studied for hours and hours.

The town at my feet now had a new dimension. I saw not only the gold-lit windows that looked upon the Tiber, some flaming cupola and the arched balcony of Palazzo Farnese, but also a town with houses and apartments and streets where people lived and worked and used their brains to communicate their thoughts to others. I discovered to my great astonishment that now I enjoyed all those subjects and books that I used to loathe when I had to go to school.

Sometimes Maria Sole would sit with me. She was preparing for the same exam but had attended her classes regularly.

"I wonder where Youssouf has ended up?" I asked.

"Why Youssouf? I suppose he's back in Albania."

"Yes, but I wonder if he is alive or dead or in prison. If it weren't for him I probably would not be here studying."

"I don't know what you are talking about," Maria Sole said, "and I can't study if you go on interrupting me."

One evening I was in the living room and an unknown boy appeared in the doorway. He had very green, rather round eyes and was dressed in the most proper, old-fashioned way I had seen in a long time.

"So this is Suni, under the lampshade," were the first words I heard him say. He had been on the Russian front with Gianni, and Gianni had asked him to visit his family when he returned to Italy. I remembered Gianni having mentioned in a letter that he had met this boy, Urbano Rattazzi, and that he thought he would make a good husband for Maria Sole.

Urbano was different from any boy I had ever met. He

was extremely polite, intelligent, and studious, lived with his father and mother in a villa on the Italian Riviera and talked about everything in precise, rather precious language. He stayed in Rome for a few days, helped me with my Greek, which he could translate on sight, and accompanied me to one of my classes on a bicycle wearing a pair of gloves and a dark hat like an English businessman's. He was a cavalry officer, spoke perfect German, loathed the Fascists and explained to me at great length that they were leading Italy to destruction.

For the first time I heard a friend talk about the Fascists as if they were different from the Italians. He came from a family of politicians.

My friends laughed at me and joked, "You can't go around with Urbano Rattazzi. That is the name of a street, not of a boy. Anyway, he walks like a cavalry officer and he speaks so seriously about everything that you can't possibly be amused." They were a little envious.

I teased Urbano because he acted so old and serious.

"Haven't you ever been in love?" I asked.

"Once," he answered gravely, "with a Madonna in the Dresden Pinakothek."

I was mystified. He went back to his villa near the sea and would write me letters in which he said I walked like Artemis and I should not have friends like Galeazzo. I didn't have time to answer. I studied and studied and swore to myself that after I had passed that exam I would read every book there was in the world.

My mother brought a hero to the house. He was a Navy officer who had sunk a British warship under extraordinary circumstances. He was tall with a very fair crew cut and cold, static, blue eyes. You never would have guessed he was Italian. He had been given the "Medaglia d'oro," the highest Italian decoration, and had refused to accept it from

Mussolini's hands. He was waiting for the King to pin it on his chest. This man resembled my ideal of a man: the modest hero. I had a schoolgirl crush on him and blushed when he came into my room to inquire about my studies.

He talked vaguely about the Navy plotting some change in the government. Everybody was plotting. It had become the national sport.

*N*ot that I had stopped seeing Raimondo. He would appear in the middle of the night, run up the three flights of stairs, stand panting at the foot of my bed saying, "*God, when will your mother put an elevator in this house?*" then lie at my feet and talk. He, too, was plotting and going around with a general who had now become the rage around town; a dark, handsome, *avventuriere* type of general who could only have been Italian. He flirted with the ladies, implied that his armored cars would protect Rome from any invasion, and was always leaving the lunch table to go and inspect some outfit in the Castelli Romani where he certainly could have gone half an hour later. He mixed toughness with *mondanité* and I am sure he pictured himself as a modern Rhett Butler.

Raimondo talked about this General Carboni of his with extreme objectivity. He would laugh about his weaknesses but still had a certain faith in his qualities and hoped he could do something for Italy. He and Galvano were all mixed up in talking to the Allies, trying to get an armistice, getting rid of the Fascists, and turning against the Germans; but, of course, it was all rather secret and we didn't discuss it much.

Instead, Raimondo would talk about his actress, how nasty she was, how much she made him suffer, how she would ask him to go to her and then refuse to see him or be in bed with somebody else, how he longed to get over this sickness which possessed him, so that we could get married. I listened. I wondered if it ever occurred to him that I might suffer, too.

Sometimes, bicycling across the town, I would go and visit him in the Grand Hotel. He had picked up a sort of monster who valeted for him, a dwarf with an enormous long head who never stopped talking about his own romantic conquests. Raimondo saw a lot of a medium who read the letters you had in your pocket, told you what would be written in tomorrow's war bulletin, lit candles from across the room, and predicted the future. The room was full of people and the usual utter confusion.

One afternoon Raimondo asked me to go and see him. I appeared at the desk of the Grand Hotel saying I was going upstairs. Lorenzo, the concierge, asked me to wait a second, rang upstairs, and told me Raimondo had gone out. I decided to leave my book satchel in his room and come back later. I walked upstairs and found the door locked, so I knew he was there. I got so mad I took my very heavy satchel and threw it with all my strength against the door, then I left and went to a public booth and called Raimondo on his private number.

"Nini," he said, "please, this poor woman who was here, she almost died with fright."

"But, why do you ask me to come when you know you are going to be in bed with somebody else?"

"Really, Nini, how could I know I was going to be in bed with this woman? Be sensible. Come and pick up your books and don't be jealous, it's not like you."

I went to pick up the books and he told me of how the

woman had trembled and cried with fright, putting on her clothes, and we ended up laughing as always.

Now and then we would dine out together but I had too much studying to do to be able to wait around for him. He had hired a taxi which he was driven around in by a crazy, bald, amusing chauffeur, Fortunato. With the taxi he would appear at strange, unexpected hours bringing laughter and chaos, disrupting everybody's life.

Maria Sole never talked much. But one afternoon after Raimondo had left and she saw tears in my eyes, she put her book down and said, "I can't understand why you go on seeing him," then went back to her book.

With Maria Sole I bicycled off in the worst state of nerves for the exams which had been moved up to the beginning of June. We were confronted with the joke of writing a paper on how the Italian Army never had and never would be beaten because the whole country was backing its soldiers. There must have been someone with a great sense of humor sitting up there in the Ministry of Education choosing subjects for the *maturità* examination.

The written examinations went on for three days: Italian, Latin, Greek; then the orals in two sessions, one week apart from one another. My first oral session was on scientific subjects and the result was a total disaster. I came home sobbing.

My mother took the situation in hand.

"You are worn out," she said, "and here you'll get worse. Take the train and go to Forte dei Marmi, stay there for a week; sleep, swim, rest, study, and come back for the next exam feeling like another person. Take your young tutor with you."

He was a Jewish boy who couldn't get a job because of racial laws and who had come to tutor me all the time I was at home. He was formidably intelligent and could teach practically every subject. He even gave me a taste for mathematics, which was my pet hate. He would comfort me when I got depressed and look at me with sad, yellowish dog's eyes.

We sat under the pine trees on the same armchair and crammed like lunatics. The last subject, history of art, we went through on the train going back to Rome. I was suntanned, rested, and in high spirits when I faced the second commission.

Exams were public, and when I walked away from the table dancing with happiness, I saw an Army officer who had been on the train the day before.

"I was so amused at the idea of your preparing the exam yesterday on a train, that I couldn't resist the temptation to see how it would turn out. I see you are happy. I am happy for you." He left and I never saw him again, nor ever knew who he was.

The results came. I had passed; so had Maria Sole. She didn't seem to really care; I was so delighted I walked down the street and thought every person I met was beautiful. I discovered shiny eyes and smiling lips and glossy skins, I discovered Rome in the sun and the heaven of having nothing to do. Now I would read, now I would become a doctor, now my life would have a meaning.

The only thorn was that I was ashamed to show my joy to my Jewish tutor.

In early 1943, Gianni had flown back from Tunisia with the officers of his regiment. They had been machine-gunned in flight, his captain had been killed, most of them wounded. He was safe and had gone back to Turin to work at Fiat. He had arrived in Rome in the middle of the night, unexpected and smiling. We had all crowded into my mother's room, Gianni in his uniform surrounded by us in our nightdresses. The maids had cried.

My Navy hero had been given his medal by the King and wore it underneath his lapel so that it wouldn't show, because everyone was supposed to stand at attention and salute when a hero went by. I asked him how it felt to be decorated on a platform in great pomp. He said the only thing he remembered was his tummyache.

In Forte dei Marmi people came whom we had never seen before: Navy officers, diplomats, old politicians. They all talked about something which was going to happen and change things, but they all had different plans and ideas and all were sworn to secrecy.

My mother decided to send my brothers and sisters to Switzerland, where they could go to school. Clara was there already with her daughter while Tassilo stayed on in Italy. We remained, my mother, Lotti, and myself to await events.

Sicily was invaded; the bombing grew worse. One was not allowed on the beach at night. The friends who used to come and stay were all soldiers or in military schools.

We were back in Rome when, on July 25, Mussolini was voted out by the "Gran Consiglio" and then arrested. Badoglio took his place. Galeazzo had voted against his father-in-law.

The people thought that by getting rid of the Fascists the war would end. But they seemed to forget two things: that it was the Fascists who were voting against Mussolini and that the Germans, our allies, could be all over Italy in a few days.

"*La guerra continua*"—the three words that Badoglio had announced on the radio on being appointed by the King to succeed Mussolini—had thrown the country into incredulous despair.

I was serving in the Air Force hospital. The wounded soldiers and officers were at a loss. Nobody knew what was going on. Everyone was afraid of being called a Fascist in a country where, to go to school or university or to become a nurse or to have a job or be an officer or be a professor, you had to have a Fascist party card. The anti-Fascists were outside Italy or in prison or confined.

In the ward one soldier pulled out a Communist party card and proceeded to give orders to everybody else. He was not popular.

For the first time Raimondo appeared in uniform. He had been appointed ADC to General Carboni. He had a car in which he drove all day long to inspect the tanks of the armored division that General Carboni was in charge of and to whom was entrusted the defense of Rome. Raimondo was tired and worried. He said the armored division was in perfect condition, the morale of the troops excellent, his General a good commander, full of guts and liked by his officers and soldiers. Then he added that nobody knew exactly what was going to happen. General Carboni was arrogantly convincing on the fact that Rome would be defended brilliantly.

More and more German soldiers appeared in the streets of Rome and on the roads going south, but, of course, they were going to defend Sicily against the Allied invasion.

I saw my hero friend, he was leaving on his destroyer. His blue eyes matched the blue ribbons of the decoration on his dark blue uniform. He was calm and handsome. I wished he would love me. He gave me a sense of strength and security. I knew he would do the right thing and now he was going away.

Communications had become so difficult in town that most of the doctors slept in the hospital. I was on night duty. In the evenings we would sit and talk; we never knew what tomorrow would bring. The doctors slept with their windows open to get some fresh air. When dawn appeared I would go and close their shutters, then make the patients' beds before I went home.

I went with Raimondo to visit Galeazzo. He was in his flat in Parioli, practically under arrest. Edda received her friends in one room and Galeazzo received his in another. It was embarrassing and difficult. Galeazzo was nervous, but pleased to see us. He mentioned, laughing (or rather sniggering), how many of his friends he had never seen or heard from since he had fallen into disgrace.

"Let's hear you who tell the truth, Suni," he challenged me. "Do you think they are going to kill me?"

I smiled to make it less terrible and answered, "Yes, I do, Galeazzo."

"And who do you think would kill me, the Germans or the Allies?"

"I'm afraid either one," I answered honestly and regretted it while I was speaking. His face turned pale.

"Remember one thing, Suni," he said. "If they kill me, they will kill you, too."

"That may well be."

I took his hand and said I thought he ought to go to Spain, leave, go away. We knew his comrades in the Air Force were ready with a plane to fly him to safety; it would have been easy for him, then, to drive to the airport. He didn't want to run away; he believed that things would turn out some way in his favor.

I kissed him good-by. It was good-by forever.

"But, why," I said to Raimondo, when we left, "why the hell doesn't he go away while he still can?"

Galeazzo had little sense of reality and was a very poor judge of human beings. I would have wanted to help him; he had so many times helped people I had asked him to intercede for when one word from him could change their future from death to life. Now he was surrounded by people who flattered him. They assured him that everybody loved him and that, certainly, his life was not in danger.

Raimondo drove me home in silence and I went back to the hospital.

I worked with the nurses of my mother's school in the pavilion of the Littorio Hospital that had been taken over by the Air Force. Now and then, when she felt lonely or useless, my mother would come and help; I discovered her making the beds of the orderlies who pretended to be sick, and teased her about it. She smiled. "Why not? Poor boys." She talked to the patients but then became so involved in all their problems that I begged her not to come back. When one boy died of peritonitis, as happened every day, she suffered as if he had been her own child. When I went home, I would sit with her and tell her about the things that had happened during the night. She was confused like everyone else and worrying about the outcome of all that was going on.

Friends who were in the Air Force would beg me to get them a sick-leave certificate from the doctors. What was the point of dying now? Sometimes I managed.

But the war did continue. The war bulletin announced that Sergeant Baldetti had shot down three Allied planes in the sky of Naples before being hit and bailing out.

Late at night the hospital door opened and a group of Air Force men walked in with, in their midst, a young, fair, good-looking boy still in his pilot's overalls. They helped him carry his parachute and seemed very concerned.

"This is Baldetti," they said, "the pilot mentioned in this morning's bulletin. He is in shock. Look after him."

The word went around the wards and everyone who could walk came out to cheer the boy who smiled, shy and exhausted.

We put him to bed; he was hungry but the kitchen was closed, so whoever had some food hidden away brought it out for him. He was very nervous. They drugged him so that he would go to sleep. He asked me to hold his hand; I sat next to his bed and held his hand. He did not sleep but dozed off from time to time, then opened his eyes and stared at me, smiling.

When I left he said, "Will you come back tonight? Promise?"

I came back but now he was not sick enough to justify my holding his hand. During the daytime he had been decorated by the Germans and proposed for decoration by the Italians. He had recovered and would be going home on leave the next day. He asked me if I would go and say good-by to him at the station; his train left at six in the evening.

The following morning Raimondo rang me at home; he sounded anxious.

"You are not to go out this afternoon," he said.

"Why?"

"I can't explain, but I forbid you to leave the house."

"I will leave the house. I'm going to the station."

"You are not. I forbid it, do you understand? I have to go now. It's important; you must not go out."

"Good-by," I said. It was September eighth.

Sergeant Baldetti was waiting for me in front of a café. He wore his gray-blue uniform with the German cross around his neck; an Air Force private stood three steps behind him, carrying his cameras. Baldetti was the perfect picture of the successful noncommissioned officer; clean, young, decorated. We didn't have much to say to one another and I was afraid that one of my head nurses might see me, because it was strictly forbidden to meet patients outside the hospital without your uniform on, and I was wearing a cotton frock.

An old woman nudged her companion. "Look, isn't that the boy who shot down the planes? His photograph was in the paper this morning."

"I don't think so," the other answered, *"questo è più bello."*

"But it must be him. Look at the decoration. It's brand-new."

We pushed on through the crowd that was sitting, carrying bundles, hurrying, lagging; it was like a market place. I clung tightly to my bicycle for fear someone would snatch it; Baldetti said he would write to me; he would never forget me. I smiled; I said he'd better go to his train now or he might risk not finding a seat; he answered that someone was there keeping a seat for him, but he'd better go as the train was about to leave. We shook hands and then he turned back and waved; I thought of how pleased his mother would be to see him arrive alive and famous.

It was as I bicycled back down the Via Nazionale that I started noticing clusters of people listening to the radio, in front of cafés, around shops; more and more people running and then stopping suddenly, puzzled. I heard the word *"armistizio"* and thought about Raimondo's telephone call; strangely, the people all seemed worried and not happy as one would have expected. I rushed back home as fast as I could pedal, the streets were full of people, there wasn't one German to be seen.

My mother said Raimondo had telephoned; he wanted

to know where I was; would I call him from the hospital; she was waiting to see what was going to happen.

I put on my uniform, went to the hospital, and found every officer, soldier, doctor, orderly gathered in the corridor. One boy whose hand had been amputated was leaning against the window, his head on his arm, sobbing. I put my hand on his shoulder. "Try to understand," he looked at me through tears, "I would have gladly given both my hands for my country." Some were happy, some were sad, but all were waiting for someone to tell them what they should do. Badoglio had announced the armistice, but his communiqué contained a cryptic phrase which urged the Italian soldiers to react if they were attacked by enemy forces. Who was the enemy? Who was going to attack? That was left for each to guess for himself.

We spent the night on the telephone. They had an Air Force exchange with direct lines out of town but whomever we rang answered the same thing: "We don't know. The only thing to do is wait."

I finally got through to Raimondo. He said, "Don't worry, everything is going to be all right; I'll come and see you as soon as I can; you'll see, everything will be all right." He repeated it so often that I knew he thought it wasn't all right at all.

The Germans were shooting, killing, occupying barracks. I came home to find it was full of *carabinieri* who had jumped the wall from their barracks at the far end of the street into our garden. They were asking for civilian clothes with which to escape capture. We didn't have many men's trousers or shirts in the house, but people from across the road, refugees from bombed areas, gave them all they had. It was pitiful to see this stream of young men throwing off their uniforms and leaving in their rolled-up shirt sleeves, pretending they were civilians. Most of them didn't know where they were going. If they had a family they went to the station and tried to get on a train that would take them near home, but otherwise they just walked the streets hoping to find somebody who would give them an order.

Raimondo came in his car; we went around Rome. Here and there were groups of soldiers fighting the Germans.

"But, I thought your General was going to defend Rome," I said. "Where is he?"

"You don't understand. The Allies were supposed to arrive. Something went wrong."

He was so tired and desperate that I didn't insist. I sat staring at the people who walked, aimless and passive, as if an earthquake had destroyed their lives.

*T*he doorbell rang. I was downstairs, opened the small door, and two men in civilian clothes came in with two suitcases. They walked into the shady entrance, where the staircase began.

"I am General Carboni," the older man said, "and this is my son." The son bowed his head. "We need refuge. We would like to stay here until we know how things will turn out. It is dangerous for us to be seen around. The Germans are capturing everybody."

My mother was walking down the stairs.

"All right, General," she said, "come in, come upstairs. I'm afraid you will have to share a room with your son. This house is not very big, you know."

"No, but it is out of the way and nobody will be looking for us in Trastevere."

Raimondo arrived in uniform. The General spoke to him with authority.

"Follow the column of the King and ask for orders. Say I am expecting orders, I want to know what I am to do."

Raimondo stood at attention, *"Sì, Signor Generale."* He put his arm around my shoulders, kissed me, and said, "I'll be back," and drove away.

He came back hours later, laughing convulsively.

"They said to tell you *'di arrangiarsi,'* to manage as best you can. You should have seen them." He was hysterical.

Raimondo calmed down, took off his boots, and told us of how he had driven like mad out of Rome on the road he knew was being traveled by the King's column to get to Pescara. He had finally reached the column at a railroad crossing which was shut. He got out of his car and rushed up looking for Badoglio. They were all there, the King, the Queen, and the generals. He had finally found the commander-in-chief.

"I am General Carboni's ADC. General Carboni is waiting for orders. He sent me to ask for orders; what is he to do?"

A few of them got out of their cars and started talking, discussing what should be done, but at that moment the train appeared. They rushed back to their cars, the gates were lifted, and the whole column drove away at full speed with Badoglio and another general hanging out of the windows, shouting, "Tell him to manage as best he can."

When he came to this point of his story, Raimondo doubled up in two and screamed, *"Di arrangiarsi;* do you understand? The cars whizzing forward and they shouting *'di arrangiaaarsi'* and waving from their windows."

He had stood, Raimondo, in the dust blown up by the wheels, then turned his car around and driven sadly back. General Carboni swallowed two or three times, said nothing, then retired to his room. Raimondo went to sleep and I went back to the hospital.

*T*he telephone operator rang up a post on some beach near Anzio, "What's happening?"

"Nothing much."

"Can you see anything?"

"Yes, some soldiers walking on the beach."

"Soldiers? Are they Allies?"

"We don't know; they might be."

He rang up again an hour later, "Well?"

"No, they seem to be Germans." Our hearts sank.

Whatever happens, a hospital is still a place where people are dying and have to be looked after, so we worked and tried to comfort the soldiers, telling them that as long as they were in the hospital they were safe.

I went home and found two more guests: Raimondo's mother, who was afraid to remain in the Grand Hotel alone, and a friend of a friend of my mother's who said he was organizing the Communist party's cadres and spent his time on the telephone. He, also, had asked to be hidden but wanted nobody to know he was there.

General Carboni, on discovering this man's arrival, begged that his presence, too, be kept secret. So they were served meals in their rooms, then would walk out on the terrace, catch a glimpse of one another, and rush back into hiding.

General Carboni approached my mother and murmured, "Don't you think there might be something between you and me, Donna Virginia? You are so charming."

"I don't see how we would find the time, General," my mother answered sweetly.

The radio announced that General Calvi di Bergolo, one of the King's sons-in-law, would take the command of Rome. General Carboni seemed relieved. The Germans were now asking everyone who belonged to the Armed Forces to show up at headquarters.

Then the door opened once again and a man I had never seen before stormed in.

"Where is your mother?" he asked. "Tell her I am Colonel Giaccone. I have just jumped off the train on which the Germans are taking my commander, General Calvi di Bergolo, off to Germany as a prisoner. I need to be hidden."

Oh God, I thought, when is this going to end? Does anyone know what is going on?

A bed was found for Colonel Giaccone, too. He also telephoned; he also wanted to be incognito. I couldn't understand why they didn't all put their heads together and try to make some sense instead of sitting in separate rooms hanging onto telephones. They were, let's face it, getting the only information they had from the maid, Jolanda, who went to the market place, and from me, because I went to the hospital.

Raimondo came and went. He still had his official car. He knew, by now, that the whole plan had failed and that he would have to find a way out for himself.

When Jolanda returned from the market, they all jumped on her: "What's happened?"

"Were there soldiers?"

"What do the people say?"

"Are the Allies coming?"

And on Jolanda's answers depended the mood of the next few hours.

General Carboni became extremely concerned about his future. It was evident that the more time went by the more difficult it would be to make a decision, so now he incessantly asked everyone the same question: "What should I do, report to Italian Headquarters, whoever that might be? Go into hiding? Try to reach the Allies going south?"

It was almost impossible to answer, as, whichever side he chose, he was not going to be particularly popular and every hour that went by made his position worse.

The moment came when, at the far end of the street, they posted a German soldier with a machine gun in his hands. A boy of about eighteen with light, terrified eyes, wearing a camouflage battle outfit. I am sure he didn't know what he was doing there. He certainly was scared stiff. Some little boys ran around him to touch his trousers that looked like leaves. He shouted them back and pointed his gun at them. The mothers pulled the children away; he pointed his gun at them, too. After that, the women and the children stood on a corner in a group, shaking their heads.

I went back home and said that a German soldier was standing at the far end of the street. That decided General Carboni; he said he would report to Headquarters. He asked Raimondo if he was going to follow him. Raimondo hesitated, he thought it was a silly thing to do; they discussed it again, Raimondo said yes, then no. Now we were all standing downstairs in the entrance to say good-by, Raimondo still in uniform.

"For the last time, Lanza," General Carboni turned to him, "are you coming with us?"

"I am sorry, Signor Generale, no."

At that moment Raimondo's mother shouted, "Raimondo!"

"What is it, Mammà?"

"Your feet. You are barefoot. You are talking to your General without any shoes on!"

"Mammà, please, my boots are tight and my feet hurt. And, anyway, who the hell cares?"

"*Arrivederci,*" said General Carboni. He walked out of the door followed by his son, who had hardly opened his mouth during his stay, and they drove away in Raimondo's car.

"They'll arrest him," Raimondo exclaimed. "Can't he see that they are bound to arrest him? I am going south."

But even that wasn't easy. By now the Germans were stopping the trains and capturing every man who was going south. Only the roads were left and these were full of military trucks that would not carry civilians.

Colonel Giaccone left on foot. He was determined and knew what he wanted. On leaving he said to me, "If you go to Switzerland, please tell Countess Calvi di Bergolo that her husband behaved like a gentleman and a soldier." Then he stormed out as he had come in. Also the Communist friend of a friend went away. There was nobody left to telephone to.

Raimondo didn't know where to go. I took him with me to the hospital and hid him in a cellar. I asked a wounded officer, who was a friend, to bring him some food, and added that Raimondo was only waiting to leave for the south.

The officer returned. "You'd better tell your friend to change his silk shirt and to take his gold bracelet off if he wants the Germans to think he is a peasant," he snorted.

When I told Raimondo, he laughed. He only had silk shirts.

I took the revolvers and hand grenades that had been left at home and gave them to the officers in the hospital.

My mother was worried. She suspected that I was hiding Raimondo somewhere and slapped one of the nurses who tried to lie about it and cover up for me.

Early in the morning I said good-by to Raimondo on the top of the Gianicolo in the piazza where the monument to Garibaldi stands. He rode a bicycle, carried a handkerchief tied onto his handlebars like a *contadino*, and still wore his silk shirt and gold bracelet. Never had he looked more like a boy than he did now; happy, riding his bicycle, going on holiday.

"Look after yourself, Nini," he said seriously. "Don't do anything silly. Don't worry about me, I'll be all right."

We kissed and he went away, smiling under the trees.

Now the house was practically empty; my mother, Lotti, myself, the maids; no one who knew what would happen next. All one's friends were hiding or going away, not answering the telephone, pretending they were not in Rome.

My mother wanted me to go to Switzerland and join my brothers and sisters.

"Come with me," she said. "Let's go and ask Maxettino for some advice. He is in the diplomatic service and must have more news than we have."

We bicycled to the hotel in the center of Rome where he was staying and asked for him.

"There is no answer on the telephone," the concierge said, "but he must be upstairs. His key is not here."

We went up to the room and knocked on the door. No
answer. We knocked on the next door of the suite and then
again on the first one. We finally heard someone stirring
inside and then the door opened and Maxettino stood
splendid and dreamy-eyed, very tall in his dressing gown.

"What are you doing here, Virginia?" he exclaimed.

"I want your advice."

"Come in," he said, "sit down. You know each other,
don't you?"

A woman had appeared, also in a dressing gown, her hair
in a halo around her face. They held hands.

"What sort of advice do you want, Virginia?"

"About what we should do."

He looked puzzled. "What do you mean, what should
you do?"

"I mean the Germans, the Allies, the armistice."

His eyes grew wider and wider. "What are you talking
about?"

"Haven't you listened to the radio?" I interrupted.

"No."

"You haven't been out since last week?"

"No."

"Well, Mammà, I think you had better explain."

A week. I was baffled. A week. These two had loved each
other for this whole week in the middle of this town. They
hadn't spoken to anyone, seen anyone; they hadn't listened
to the radio; they didn't care about anything but one
another. They didn't know that everyone out there was torn
to shreds by doubt, hesitation, indecision; that people were
dying, being killed, deported; that the future was being
played every moment and they were lying in each other's
arms and knew only this room, this moment, this reality. I
never envied anyone more.

n Lausanne my sisters were waiting for me. Maria Sole stayed with Clara near the lake at Ouchy, and I would share a small apartment with Cristiana.

I asked to be admitted to the first year of medicine. Maria Sole had already been admitted to *chimie*.

At Red Cross Headquarters in Rome they had asked me to get in touch with the Princess of Piedmont and convey the faithful spirit of those who had remained behind. I also had a letter.

I got permission from Swiss authorities to visit Princess Marie José at a mountain place where she was residing with the children incognito, in hiding. A lady in waiting met me at the station. She was old and wearing black, sad and bewildered in that cold, wet, leafy, Swiss autumn. We went up to the hotel where they were staying. I waited in a brown *pension*-looking sitting room, getting more and more depressed, until the Princess of Piedmont arrived.

She was very beautiful and as shy as ever, her very light gaze lost in some distant dwelling.

I curtsied, kissed her hand, gave her the letter, and delivered the message. She smiled sadly and said, "Thank you" two or three times. I asked her to transmit to Countess Calvi the message from Colonel Giaccone. She seemed surprised.

Then, suddenly, with great effort, she asked, "Do you know where His Majesty is?"

I was so stunned, I murmured, "Well, yes. In the south."

Then, shy and embarrassed, we sat for a few minutes in silence before she got up and left.

I had to wait for the train to take me back to Lausanne, so the lady in waiting took me in to see the children. They were the dream of any photographer who wants to take snapshots of royal children: four; very close in age, beautiful, wearing light-colored sweaters, and in exile.

They were doing their homework. The lady in waiting
gave them lessons and she showed me proudly that the fair,
blue-eyed Prince of Naples, sitting at the little wicker table
at the foot of his bed, was drawing an Italian flag.

Cristiana went to school. In the mornings we both rushed
out to catch our trolleybuses that carried us uptown. For
lunch Clara and Maria Sole joined us, and we ate mostly
corn flakes and milk that you could buy without food
coupons, then we went back to school.

In the evenings after a hot bath, we would sit under the
covers in the big bed, Cristiana and I, and drink boiling
soup to keep ourselves warm during the night. She was full
of beaux and I would write marvelous love letters for her as,
anyway, I had nobody to write to.

News trickled in. My Navy hero had taken his destroyer
to the Spanish coast, disembarked all his sailors and officers,
and then sunk his ship. He and his crew were now in prison
in neutral Spain. I got news that Raimondo had reached
Brindisi, that Topazia's mother had been arrested by the
Germans, that Cini had been deported to Dachau, that
Italy had become an incomprehensible muddle.

More and more Italians came through the border,
walking into Switzerland at night. They were put into
camps or into requisitioned hotels and only allowed to
attend the university if they proved their serious interest in
studying and had somebody who vouched for them.

The situation deteriorated. The Swiss disliked all the
Italians and one could see their point as this whole lot of
people pouring into their country had to be fed on the
reserves they had made for themselves and no one knew
how long the war would last. The Jews disliked the
non-Jews and considered they should have stayed in Italy as
they were not risking their lives. All of them disliked

whoever had some money and could live out of a camp or had come into Switzerland legally. For some reason, these were considered traitors.

I studied. I drew amœbas and chromosomes, pistils and leaves; I spent hours writing out the results of chemistry analyses and experiments in physics, trying not to think about the world around me.

Sundays were the worst. We would have lunch at Clara's apartment after Mass and a dismal walk on the Quai d'Ouchy. The lake was silver-gray and flat, the mountains on the opposite side were beginning to show snow on their sides, and even the seagulls seemed bored. Clara managed to cook a good lunch and, with her coupons, bought each of us a salted bun filled with fresh butter, which we ate religiously. Sometimes we would go to the movies; otherwise I would walk and wish desperately for Monday to come or for something, anything, to happen.

Emilio Pucci rang up from a hospital near the border. He had escaped from prison, had been tortured by the Germans; his head had been cracked open. He had tried to bring Ciano's diary into Switzerland; they had interned him in a hospital. . . . The telephone went "click," then dead, and I didn't hear from him again. He wrote days later: he wasn't allowed to telephone or see anyone, he was tutoring in some boys' school in the countryside; would I try to get a permit to come and see him? He was desperate.

I knew the counselor to the Italian Legation in Berne and asked him to help me do something about Emilio. He managed an appointment with the Chief of Police, who

knew my mother, and I took a train to Berne wearing one
shoe and one snowboot because my chilblains were so
painful I couldn't walk with my right shoe on. My sisters
and I decided this was the best solution, as two snowboots
might seem disrespectful to a Swiss official.

He was extremely kind but could do nothing for Emilio,
who would have to stay in the school under a false name as
a tutor and be thankful that, under extremely dangerous
circumstances, he was safe and looked after. Later on the
official might give me a permit to visit Emilio. I said,
"Thank you."

Giorgio B., the legation counselor who had accompanied
me, took me to his home for lunch and then to the station.
As the train was about to leave he handed me a ticket. It
entitled me to travel first class instead of second. I was very
touched, not because I cared at all about the red velvet
seats, but it was such a long time since anyone had been
kind to me that I was moved to tears. I became devoted to
Giorgio B.

I wrote him long letters and sent him stories; he would
ring me and tell me if he liked them or not. It was an *amitié
amoureuse*. I loved having someone to talk to, to feel in touch
with. We could discuss the situation in Italy, what would
happen, the future. He gave me news that he got through
the Vatican's diplomatic pouch, I gave him my despair.

The day came when Galeazzo was tried, then sentenced,
then shot in the back while tied to a chair in a courtyard of
Verona. I could not talk to my fellow students about being
struck by Ciano's death. They all hated him; he was the
symbol of fascism; they all said it served him right. I saw
him as Galeazzo, a friend, weak and good, credulous and
childishly vain. I imagined him disbelieving to the last,
hoping in some magic charm that would save him. Giorgio
B. understood. I could at least tell him I was sad.

I went to chemistry lab and stood, as always, next to a French boy called Jacques. We boiled strange liquids in glass tubes, smelled fumes, watched the changing colors, added poisonous drops, tried to guess what the powder we had been given was made of.

Jacques was strong and very, very French. He wore a thick sweater, like that of a mountain guide, over his shirt and was extremely serious about his studies.

We wrote the results of our analyses on a big sheet of checkered paper and compared notes every few minutes, joking. He passed me his sheet of paper and indicated three words written on the upper side. Prepared to laugh, I read *"Je t'aime,"* and the laughter died in me as I looked at his tense face, his clenched jaw. I blushed.

"Have you no reaction?" He shook me by the shoulder.

"Réaction rouge," I wrote on my sheet using the chemistry terminology, not wanting to hurt him, not wanting to lose his companionship, not wanting to lie to him.

I felt so old. I was one year older than he was and he seemed an eternity away. How could I explain?

walked down the stairs into Place de l'Université as classes ended. Dusk made the square gray, there was a slight mist in the air. I saw a woman walking toward me, the figure of a plump girl with a drawn, terrified face.

"Are you Suni Agnelli?" she asked.

"Yes."

"I must talk to you at once; it is important, it is urgent. We can't talk in the middle of the street. Give me your home address, I will come and see you."

I was slightly anxious as I waited for this strange woman. She arrived, sat on a chair, and as she spoke she clenched her hands, shaking.

"My name is Hilde B.," she said. "I am German, I work for the SS."

Sweat covered my whole body.

"I was in charge of Galeazzo Ciano until his death," she continued. "I got him a vial of potassium cyanide. They had sworn to me that it would work. He did not die, he was only sick, so they had to practically carry him to the execution." She sobbed for one second, then continued, "Galeazzo told me about you. I was with him all the time he was in prison in Verona. I was supposed to make him talk; instead I became fond of him. I wanted to help him, to try to arrange his escape—at least to spare him the execution. I didn't even manage that." She broke down again. "You must help me," she ended.

God, I prayed, help me, and said, "Yes, what can I do?"

"Get me a vial of real cyanide, one which will kill me instantly, one which you will guarantee is going to kill me instantly. I have to go back to Italy. If the Germans discover me, if they kill me I don't care, but if they torture me—I know what it means—I know I will not be able to resist, I can't face it. I know you study medicine. I know you can get it. Please get it for me, do it for Galeazzo."

I swallowed. Where was I going to get cyanide?

"But, why don't you ask the Swiss for asylum?" I asked. "They won't refuse now that you are here, if you explain."

"I can't," she murmured, "my husband is a general on the Russian front."

I went to an Italian Jewish boy who was assistant to the chemistry professor and told him I must have a killing dose of cyanide potassium in a vial, immediately, for a woman who might be tortured. She was a partisan, I lied. Together we went at night to the laboratory, filled the vial, sealed it, and Hilde got it.

I would wake up at night wondering about the vial.

Months went by. Monotonous, cold Swiss months. Lausanne is a town where, if you walk through the Place Saint François and up the Rue du Bourg four times a day, you end up by knowing every face you meet. When we sat at the lunch table with my sisters we would announce new arrivals to one another: "A middle-aged Italian who looks quite nice"; "Two young French boys"; then, as spring approached, "Six Americans." These were pilots who had bailed out over Switzerland or prisoners who had escaped. They wore a brownish battle dress with a little flag on their breast. The others wore their little flag on their civilian jacket and would cover it up holding a book over it with their arm bent in a nonchalant fashion.

In my class I discovered that one boy was Italian months after we sat on the same bench and only because I asked one day, "How come you have such an Italian name?"

He was a Jew and ashamed. I realized that many others behaved in the same way.

"Why don't you go back to Italy and fight the Germans?" I would argue with them. "Italy is full of partisans who are risking their lives. You only have to walk back across the border and join them instead of sitting here in school talking about how you are going to rebuild our country after the war."

Another argument arose when they circulated a petition against the Germans who had occupied the University of

Oslo and I refused to sign it and urged the other Italian boys who were in our school not to sign it. I didn't think that any Italian studying in a neutral country, when he could have been fighting at home, was in a position to sign petitions.

"It's easy for you to talk, you are not a Jew!" they screamed.

A battle of words and shouts brought every Italian in the university into the argument and the *recteur* sent a message that if we did not stop, he would prevent us from going to class. I became the most hated girl in the school.

"When the war ends, we will never allow an Agnelli to come back to Italy," they said. "You are Fascist."

I said, "You are cowards."

At that time my mother was arrested by the Germans and was at the San Gregorio Clinic. She asked us please to make no move to help her; it would only make things worse. I would telephone Giorgio B. He was kind and sweet and would comfort me assuring me that things would turn out all right. The Germans had arrested so many ladies in Rome and sent them to the San Gregorio Clinic that one shouldn't fear the worst.

Partisans would appear now and then, friends of ours who fought with the brigades in the mountains and would come to Switzerland to find contacts or receive orders. They were nervous and fanatic. Underground war is a mixture of mystery, lying, heroism, waiting, killing, and terror. To survive and still be a man you have to be extremely tough.

They would bring us news of other friends, those who had been killed or deported, those who were fighting with the Allies, the few who were fighting with the Germans. When they first told me that Urbano Rattazzi was with the Germans I couldn't believe it. I thought there must be some mistake. But then I heard he had become Valerio Borghese's ADC and was fighting with the "Decima Mas" on the Anzio beachhead against the Allies. He was the last person I would have expected to be on the Fascist side.

It was difficult to understand the mechanism that had been triggered in people's brains by the chaos of September the eighth.

My mother had been released after an operation on her tonsils. She would try to come to Switzerland soon. The news we got was incomplete, fragmentary, contradictory.

At last we heard she would be arriving at the border and catching the ten-thirty train. I went to meet her and sat in the train with her in the middle of sullen strangers, unable to find the words to say the only thing that made any sense: that I loved her.

Instead, when she pulled out of her bag a gold photograph holder that opened into seven frames with the snapshot of one of her children in each and I saw the monogram of the SS engraved on it, I covered her hands.

I scolded her, "Please, Mammà, please. Put it away and don't pull it out again because, here, you are going to get into real trouble."

She wanted to explain.

I whispered, "Later, later," and we remained silent. Whatever we tried to say was difficult, like people coming from two different worlds.

When we arrived at the Lausanne station, we saw that a special edition of the newspapers announced that Rome had been liberated by the Allies without one shot being fired. The Germans had left without defending Rome.

My mother burst out crying. "Thank God!" she said, "thank God."

I put my arm around her shoulders, my brave, young, frail mother, and we walked home.

She told me then, but with infinite discretion and reserve, that General Wolff had asked her to mediate an interview between the Pope and himself so as to allow Rome to be saved from mining or fighting. When she had succeeded, he had given her the photograph holder as a sign of gratitude.

I wanted to leave. I wanted to go back to Italy. When one is young one thinks about oneself most of the time. So I would sit planning which would be the best way. I went to the border on the Lake of Lugano and an Italian gentleman promised to get me through the wire net that the Germans had strung across the frontier. He organized most of the partisans' arrivals and departures.

Gianni, who in the meantime had been made vice-president of Fiat, came to visit my mother as he had an official German permit. He and I decided that we would go south, cross the lines, and join the Allies. First I would have to smuggle myself into Italy.

We chose a small village near the border, where I was to meet him at three o'clock the next Wednesday, and he went back to Turin.

My mother was worried but agreed that we should go. She was sad. That atmosphere of Switzerland depressed her as much as it did me.

I said good-by, thinking of what was waiting for me and not of what I was leaving behind.

Part Four

spent the night in the villa of the Italian gentleman who organized the smuggling of people across the border. It was all very mysterious and even meals had a flavor of conspiracy. One pretended not to know why the other people were there or what they were doing. They talked instead about the weather with an undercurrent of danger in every word. I would certainly make the worst possible conspirator, so I walked across the garden, down to the lake, and watched the water while I thought about the strangeness of human behavior. I was beginning to notice how childish grown-up people were and wondered why children are always made to believe that all adults are reasonable. Age and intelligence have nothing to do with one another.

The next morning somebody drove me to a farmhouse where a large family was leading its everyday life. The mother was cooking, the two boys working in the fields, the younger children playing around, the girls cleaning up. They gave me a chair and I sat in my blue pleated skirt, white shirt, and blue cardigan, rather like a schoolgirl waiting to be called to the blackboard. The mother would look at me from time to time and shake her head.

Because of the mysterious atmosphere, I really had no idea of what would happen to me or how I would get across the border. I had paid some money and they said they would get me through. I waited and became frightened because I heard the boys say to one another that today the soldiers weren't behaving as usual and probably it would be impossible to cross.

I panicked. What would Gianni do if he arrived and didn't find me? I had no way of communicating with him and I wouldn't know how to arrange another date. I got up and asked the boys what was happening.

They shrugged their shoulders. "If it's not today, you'll go tomorrow."

"It's impossible!" I was dying of anguish. "They are waiting for me."

"So? What do you want to do, get killed by the Germans?"

My throat went dry.

"I must go," I repeated.

"After lunch we'll try," and they went back to their work.

I watched the mother, who was preparing the sauce to pour over the *polenta*. She had cooked some birds and was picking the meat off their little bones and throwing it inside a saucepan where it turned into a dark, thick gravy.

Time for lunch came and we all sat around a big table. They ate hungrily and kept on pushing the large plate toward me saying, "Eat, eat. You'll need it. Over there you will have no food."

I couldn't swallow, I tried to smile. The mother kept on shaking her head at me.

"All right, let's try," one boy said sleepily when lunch was over, and we walked off, the two boys and myself.

We walked through the woods until we could see the tall wire net in front of us; we crouched and waited until we heard two men speaking German, then their voices dying away. One boy had a big pair of pliers with a cutting edge. He cut out a piece of net and then beckoned to me.

"Go, now," he said.

I lay on my stomach and slipped through. My cardigan caught onto the wire, ripped, and when I got up the bells went, "Ding, ding, ding."

I leaped across the stretch of grass in front of me and fell on the ground behind a tree, my heart somersaulting against my ribs. Nothing happened.

I got up, brushed my clothes with my hands, walked to

the road, and down to the village which I now saw was not far away. My watch said a quarter to two; I had an hour before our meeting time. Then I saw the clock on the church tower with the hands marking ten to three and I remembered that, of course, between Italy and Switzerland there was an hour's time difference.

Two German soldiers were walking up the road. They said, "Hello," gaily waving their hands, and I answered, "Hello," laughing as I walked quickly down the road so as not to be late.

I thought, What will I do if Gianni is not here? I had no money, no papers.

Then I saw a car coming past the last houses of the village and into the open. I walked to the center of the road and waved. When Gianni saw me he swerved the car from one side of the road to the other in a mad slalom until he stopped in front of me and laughed.

*G*ianni had brought Maner Lualdi, who was a friend. He was a pilot and, since he was in military uniform, had evidently joined the Fascists. Gianni drove me to Laveno, where my cousin Berta had a house on Lake Maggiore, and said he would pick me up the next day.

He came back. Berta had given me a skirt and two shirts, we waved good-by and drove off.

In the late afternoon we were going up the road to the Porretta Pass when we saw a car burning on the side of the road. After a mile or two we met another car, and another, in flames.

"How strange," Gianni said.

Then we realized that an Allied aeroplane was machine-gunning every car moving up that road and had evidently, by mere chance, missed us. The day was ending as we drove into Florence.

It was full of young, boisterous, scared Fascist officers. They carried their machine guns and put their hand grenades on the table while they were eating.

The boys wore black polo-neck sweaters under their jackets and had lots of badges on their uniform collars, sleeves, and fronts. They looked rather like a ballet troupe preparing a performance about the war.

Somebody asked Gianni, "What do you think of the *'repubblichini?'* " He meant the Fascist sympathizers of Mussolini's tottering "Republic" at Salò.

"Poor devils," Gianni answered.

We were planning to drive to a farm that our grandfather owned near Perugia and hide there until the Allies liberated that part of the country. It seemed only a matter of days now. The Allies were advancing, even if very slowly, up the center of Italy and Monte Corona was practically on the front line.

We hid our papers. I had my nurse's pass inside the pocket of my uniform in Gianni's suitcase. We carried two forged cards on which we appeared as brother and sister by the name of Gino and Sandra Antari. The director of Fiat in Florence was a young, clever, and efficient man who organized our departure. We changed cars and took a very small dark blue Fiat station wagon. The back part was entirely filled with tanks of gas. A German sergeant in civilian clothes would accompany us to Monte Corona and in exchange would have the car for himself to drive north. A car, then, was as precious as diamonds and the Germans were already thinking of how they could get away from the front to escape being taken prisoners.

We left when darkness fell. The roads going south were cluttered with military vehicles. I think ours was the only civilian car driving toward the front. The German was very authoritative, a real sergeant. He insisted on driving the car himself because, otherwise, he said, they would stop us.

He drove very badly. The three of us were squeezed in the two front seats. Gianni would nudge me, sighing when the German suddenly stepped on the brakes without any reason or accelerated at an intersection. Two or three times they tried to stop us. German soldiers with a metal plaque hanging around their necks, like the wine *sommeliers* in French restaurants, stood at crossroads controlling papers and cars. Our German would bounce out of the car, run up to the soldier with his fists in the air, and pour out a torrent of German words. I can't think what he said but they let us through every time. There were only Germans on the road. The columns were interminable. We decided to take a side road where there might be less traffic.

We had to make progress while it was dark, as in daytime our car would have been noticeable and we risked having it snatched by somebody. We drove on a road that ran parallel to a canal. The German was very tired, he rubbed his eyes now and then because of the strain of driving in the dark. Gianni tried once more to convince him to let him take the wheel. The German refused.

Then I heard Gianni shout, *"Attento! Attento!"* just before the car turned over and we rolled into the canal. I had my hand outside the window holding onto the roof to keep my balance in the middle of the two seats. I felt my hand crack as the car hit bottom.

There was very little water, we crawled out.

"Did you hurt yourself?" Gianni asked anxiously.

"I must have broken my hand. You?"

"My foot is falling off."

I looked at his leg. It was true, his ankle had split and the bone was falling into his sock. He was lying on the ground wet and helpless.

"Che coglione," he murmured, "what a fool. I knew it, I told him."

We had to find someplace to carry Gianni to. Not a car came by. I saw a small house down the road. I walked to it with the German, who hadn't a scratch on his body, and knocked on the door asking for help.

When they heard the German speak they refused to open the door. I asked him to go back to Gianni and called again to the people in the house.

"Please," I said, "please, open the door. We have had an accident. My brother is hurt, he is an Italian boy, he is wet. Let him lie down in your house while I look for help."

In the end they opened the door. Gianni hopped in, he lay on the floor and when they saw him they lit a fire to dry his clothes. He was shivering and his lips were blue. I started to cry and Gianni put his finger to his lips and signaled with his head that I shouldn't behave like that.

"My hand hurts," I excused myself.

He smiled. I could see he was in terrible pain but he didn't say a word.

We had to find a hospital. The people said there was one in Foiano della Chiana a few miles away, but I couldn't think how we would get him there. Our car was lying upside down in the canal and nobody went by. So we left, the German and I, walking arm in arm into the night looking for someone who would carry Gianni to the hospital.

We finally saw a car on the side of the road with two German soldiers asleep in the front seat. My German talked to them but they did not answer. He pulled the one who had his head on the wheel by the hair and held his head up while he explained what he wanted. The boy opened his eyes and listened, then when his head was let go, it fell back on the wheel like a fruit off a tree and he went back to sleep.

We walked again. I carried Gianni's briefcase with many one-thousand-lire notes as big as sheets of paper in it, as I hadn't dared leave it with him in his condition. We met another car, more soldiers asleep. It took us time to find one who, in exchange for money, agreed to come and fetch Gianni.

We drove him to the hospital. It was dawn when we reached the entrance. Two old, very thin women dressed in dirty white uniforms brought a stretcher to carry Gianni in.

"D'you think they'll manage?" he joked with me. "They must be ninety."

They put his stretcher on the floor in the corridor where other wounded people lay, and then left.

The German told me he would try to get the car onto the road and drive back to Florence. If he succeeded, he would report to Fiat about what had happened.

I said good-by.

*T*here was no electricity. The noise of cannonading, shelling, and bombing was very close. The Allies were expected from day to day. The front must have been a few miles away, which explained the worn-out German soldiers who were too tired even to try to escape. They must have come from battle.

I asked for a doctor. They said he was sleeping—he was exhausted, he had operated all the previous day and all night, we couldn't disturb him. Gianni was shivering again, they put a blanket over him. Hour after hour went by; he never complained until he pulled at my skirt and said, "Please, Suni, do something! I can't stand it any longer."

I went into the room where the doctor was asleep. He sat up in his bed. He had a round head with almost shaved grayish hair. He stared at me. I asked him to come and see my brother; his foot was falling off, he was in pain.

He said there was nothing he could do about it. There was no water, no electricity, no medicines.

I closed the door behind me and looked him straight in the eyes.

"Listen," I said, "we are trying to cross the lines. My brother's name is Giovanni Agnelli. He is the vice-president of Fiat. We are traveling under false names. You can go and denounce us to the Germans, or you can try to save his leg."

He put his hand over his shaved head and rubbed it up and down.

"Let me think about it," he said.

Then he came to see Gianni. "I'm alone," he said. "Who'll give him anesthesia if I operate on him?"

"I am a nurse," I murmured, terrified.

"All right, we'll operate, but we must wait until I can get the generator working so that I can have an X-ray."

They gave Gianni a shot of some useless drug, but now we knew what we were waiting for.

I put the mask over Gianni's face and held the chloroform bottle in my hand as I had seen it done in the operating theater. Before I started pouring the contents into the hole of the mask Gianni wriggled his fingers in a sign of salute. I was scared I would give him too much chloroform and he wouldn't wake up again, so now and then he would move and the doctor said, "Give him more."

He took the whole of Gianni's anklebone out and then sewed his foot up again. The doctor was very pleased with his operation and I was very pleased that Gianni was still alive.

We put him into a bed and I prayed that the Allies would arrive.

*G*ianni woke up and moaned. *"Mineral wasser,"* he begged over and over again. He tossed and turned his head from one side to the other. I held him down on the bed.

The two old women were the only women nurses in the hospital and the hospital was more of a market place than anything else. I think that everyone who still lived around that part of Val di Chiana had decided that the safest place to wait for the Allies was the hospital, and there they all took refuge with one excuse or another. They sat on the stairs, stood in the corridors, crowded the entrance.

The doctor, Professor Cirillo, was an exceptional character. He looked hard and stern, his face rather like a seal's with small eyes and pudgy cheeks. He was so kind I never stopped saying to myself how lucky we had been to find him. He would come into the room, put his hand on Gianni's forehead, smile at me, and say, "He'll be all right."

I tried to find out what was happening outside. I looked out onto the road: it was full of German cars and tanks and trucks and ambulances, soldiers walking in between the vehicles, all trying to go north. The German Army was certainly in retreat but it was difficult to understand where the Allies were and how long it would take them to get here. The shelling sounded near; the Germans looked haggard. That was the only clue I got.

Gianni ran a high fever. His wound was festering,

antibiotics had not been discovered. (The Allies had penicillin but not the Germans, and we hardly knew of its existence.) I sat next to his bed.

"What news?" he would ask with great effort.

"They say the Allies will be here soon."

"Do you believe it?"

"I don't know."

I heard a certain excitement in the corridor. Two young men in civilian clothes were walking into all the rooms. It was so unexpected to see men wearing suits and ties that they created a sensation.

They walked into the room where Gianni was.

"Here he is, at last," they said and my heart bounced.

They turned to me, "We have come with an ambulance to take you to Florence." They were two Fiat engineers.

"Not back to Florence, now." I was worried, disappointed.

They went up to Gianni, *"Avvocato,"* they pleaded, "you must come with us, it is too dangerous for you to stay here. In a few more days it will be impossible to get on the road. We found this ambulance with unbelievable difficulty because the Germans are requisitioning them all. You must go to a hospital where they can look after you properly."

"All right," Gianni said, feverish and in pain.

I feebly tried to resist, to say that now that we had come this far what was the point of going back. They convinced me on the grounds of Gianni's rising temperature and the total uncertainty as to when the Allies would actually arrive. It might be a day, a week, more—who could tell?

At that moment another man in civilian clothes came running up the stairs. "The Germans," he cried, "have seized the ambulance. They say they need it and have requisitioned it for military purposes."

Once more I pleaded with Professor Cirillo. Once more

without any display of emotion he walked downstairs, spoke to the Germans, and got them to tear up the order of requisition, then said, "I think the sooner you leave, the better. This might happen again and the next time we might not be so lucky."

So we laid Gianni on the stretcher and crowded into the very small ambulance. We also had aboard a poor old semi-idiotic German soldier wearing a helmet; he was supposed to stop the Germans from trying to snatch the ambulance.

I said good-by to Professor Cirillo with tears in my eyes. I hope he understood how grateful I would always be.

We drove off and then waited for darkness before we took the road north. As long as there was light the machine-gunning by the aeroplanes was continuous. Then we inserted ourselves into a military column and proceeded at a snail's pace up the one road that led to Florence. Every ten minutes there was a halt. German soldiers would peer into the ambulance. I was the only woman to be seen anywhere; we were the only civilians in the column.

Gianni grew hotter and hotter. Twice they parachuted flares that would light the whole sky up, then threw bombs. The soldiers left the cars and threw themselves in the ditch on the side of the road. I sat next to Gianni. We couldn't carry him inside a ditch with the stretcher so we waited, hoping the car wouldn't be hit.

When the trees of the Viale Michelangelo emerged into the pale dawn and we drove up the alley to the Istituto Ortopedico Toscano on the outskirts of Florence, it was as if we had traveled one year.

The two Fiat engineers who had risked their lives said good-by politely and left. I took a shower and enjoyed the water on my skin.

We had a big room with two beds and a window looking out on the park. At the end was Viale Michelangelo. Many doctors came in to see Gianni. They all agreed that the operation had been excellent even though the wound on his foot was festering. They dressed it and gave him medicines but he had to lie in bed and still ran a temperature.

I asked a doctor to look at my aching hand. They X-rayed it and discovered two fractured bones and put my fingers in traction with a complicated system of wires. When Gianni woke up and saw it he laughed. "What is this bird's cage they've put on you?" and then he asked if my broken hand hurt.

There was a dressing gown in Gianni's suitcase, a red-plaid man's dressing gown. I put it on because it was difficult to slip any sleeve over my cage.

One afternoon Gianni said with infinite melancholy, "I wonder if you could manage not to wear that dressing gown? It reminds me of someone who used to wear it. It stirs up a strange feeling in me."

He was apologetic and embarrassed at being moved by something sentimental, which he considered cheap. I took it off. It was the only time he mentioned being involved with a woman.

The days were interminable. I had nothing to read. I would write and then tear up what I had written. I went for short walks in the park but as it was not to be known that Gianni was in Florence, the less people saw of me the better.

The Germans were sending all the Fiat people up north with spare parts and machinery. They did not know that what was carried out of Florence was deposited in a villa a few miles away. Even the director pretended to leave for Turin and went into hiding. He came to say good-by and told us that until the Allies arrived he would keep contact with us through his secretary.

Waiting is exhausting and nerve-racking and if to boredom you add waiting, it is killing.

Gianni talked very little. He had always hated being in a handicapped situation, and not being able to move out of his bed sent him into a sullen reverie. He would ask me for news; I had none to give. The doctors would report what they heard of Allied progress, but even they hardly left the hospital for fear of being picked up by the Germans.

One night they bombed the hospital, and the next day they moved us to a *pensione* facing the Ponte Vecchio on the north side of the Arno. Then the Germans gave orders that, as they would blow up every bridge into Florence except the Ponte Vecchio, all the houses near the Ponte Vecchio should be immediately evacuated. They were to be mined and destroyed so that the debris would prevent the Allies from driving through.

By now there wasn't one ambulance left in the whole of Florence. They carried Gianni on a kind of coffin mounted on two enormous wheels with hooded men pushing it. The weird vehicle came out of the Misericordia Museum, where they used to exhibit the means of transport adopted for the sick throughout the centuries. Because of the emergency, these had to be used.

The people in the street thought the hooded men were pushing a coffin and stood at attention; the women crossed themselves. I walked behind hoping no one would recognize me in the crowded midday Via Tornabuoni.

They had miraculously managed to find a room for us in the Blue Sisters Clinic. The nuns would give us no food, but we were thankful to have a bed. An old woman came in the morning to bring us something to eat and wash our things. Gianni imitated her broad Tuscan accent saying, *"Oh via,"* and talked to her about the war. She said the Allies would arrive next year.

But now the shiver went over the town. One felt that "liberation" was near.

Florence had become a sort of no man's land. A few Fascist and German sharpshooters, two hundred it was said, had occupied rooms here and there in the houses on the outside circle of the town and shot at whoever appeared on the streets in front of them. The people only moved in the center of town where they were out of range of the sharpshooters. Water was scarce and had to be gathered at the wells. I spent hours every day at a well in a garden near the clinic pulling up buckets of water and pouring it into the women's jugs and pails.

"You are a Communist, aren't you?" an old woman whispered to me one day. "You are good."

I laughed. "I wear a red shirt, but I am not a Communist."

She stroked my hair with faith and tenderness. "You are a Communist," she repeated.

All the young women you met in the streets wore Red Cross badges around their arms as it was said the Germans would not bother nurses. The Germans must have been surprised at this sudden population of nurses.

I now met a few friends. They were all working for the CLN, which was the Italian Resistance. They distributed sheets of paper with the news from "Radio Londra" to the people waiting at the water queues.

At dusk a friar pushed a cart around the town picking up the dead. He carried a bell in his hand and dangled it producing an absurd and tragic chime. The corpses were piled one on top of the other, one bleeding head hanging outside the cart leaving a long line of red drops. They said that at the cemetery all the coffins left unburied were bursting in the heat.

Doctors were hiding. The Germans were taking them north. Gianni was looked after by old Professor Palagi, whose fingers had been destroyed by X-rays. He would walk to the clinic in his white doctor's coat and dress Gianni's wound with what remained of his hands. It was getting better but the infection was still alive—so was the fever.

One morning the nuns called and asked me if I would carry a Red Cross flag in front of a stretcher to a street in the firing range of a sharpshooter. A woman, in advanced pregnancy, had walked out of the door to see if her husband was returning from the outskirts of Florence where he was trying to get some vegetables for her. She had been shot and had died in the clinic into which she had been carried, and once dead, the nuns would not keep her body here.

If I walked in front with a Red Cross flag, the novices would carry the stretcher with the dead woman on it.

I agreed. I pulled my nurse's uniform out of the suitcase and wore it for the first time since I had left Rome.

We walked. When we came to the intersection I waved the flag, then walked around the corner and on the sidewalk up the street to the indicated door. I could hear the girls behind me chattering their teeth and mumbling prayers while they carried the heavy stretcher. Most Italian houses have big doors that open onto a corridor-like entrance which leads to a courtyard. This entrance was full of people and the door only half open. We slid inside.

The woman's mother was crying and moaning, "What will he say? What will her husband say when he comes back? He went to fetch some vegetables for her."

There was nothing we could answer.

We left and met two partisans around the corner of the

street. They wore red, white, and green armbands and carried machine guns.

"Could you do us a favor, Sister?" they asked. "Could you go to the last house on the street you have just come from, up the stairs to where the window is half open—it should be on the third floor—and open the shutters wide so we will know that nobody is inside there?"

I was slightly astonished. "Why don't you go and see for yourselves?" I asked.

"They would shoot us; we are partisans. But they will not shoot you."

"They just shot that pregnant woman whose body we carried back."

"Oh, well, you are afraid. It doesn't matter."

I turned on my heels, walked up the street, keeping near the wall on the side of the window, into the deserted entrance, up the stairs, into the apartment on the third floor where the door had been left wide open.

In one room, lying around in extreme disorder, were empty liquor bottles, hand grenades, and bullets. I went to the window and opened the shutters wide. Then I filled my pocket with bullets and put two hand grenades inside the top of my uniform. I walked back and handed them to the partisans.

"I thought you might need these," I said. "Anyway, don't worry. You needn't be afraid. Nobody is there now."

Still the Allies did not come. The Germans were leaving, those who had no means of transportation went through Florence on foot. A small group of young boys, some of them bandaged or limping, hanging onto one another, walked down the streets. The people watched them, their shoulders against the wall, hating them in silence.

Now and then a car would rattle down the empty streets. One heard it from far away until the beige camouflaged vehicle full of tired, drawn, desperate boys drove past, and the sadness in those haggard eyes remained with you. Nothing is so heartbreaking as a beaten army in retreat, even if the retreat of the Germans meant liberation and, hopefully, for most, the end of the war.

One of the fantastically uniformed false nurses (she wore a white-and-blue checkered dress with an embroidered apron that she must have worked on for days during the long wait for the Allies) asked me to go and help at the hospital. The partisans had organized an empty ward in which to hospitalize their casualties. The underground movement was beginning to appear publicly and to menace those who had collaborated with the Fascist Republic.

When I first arrived there was only one wounded boy in the ward. He was seriously injured. A young doctor and the checkered-dress nurse were running around him, they stuck a big needle into his thigh trying to give him a hypodermoclysis, the liquid did not descend, they became nervous, another costumed woman came to help.

I stood on one side.

"You haven't cut the vial on top," I said. "It will never descend."

They were annoyed but, after a moment of embarrassment, said, "Of course, we forgot."

"This boy is very sick," I added. "Why don't you get a proper doctor from downstairs? You have no way of looking after wounded people here: no medicines, no surgical instruments, no dressings. What are you going to do?"

"We are partisans," they said proudly. "Downstairs, they worked with the Fascists. We don't want them."

I was silent. The boy got worse. They said that perhaps I had better call a doctor.

I went downstairs; everyone was in the operating theater. I called the head nurse who immediately looked at me suspiciously.

"Who are you?"

"I am a nurse," I said.

"Another one? There are dozens of unknown false nurses around. What do you want now?"

"I am a real nurse. They have a wounded boy upstairs. He is very sick. Could someone come up and look after him?"

"Why don't they bring him to the regular ward instead of making all this fuss?"

They came to an agreement. I was sent out to a private clinic where a surgeon, I think Jewish, had had his appendix taken out to avoid being carried north. I asked him to come to the hospital because the partisans needed him. He followed me. The streets were dangerous because of the sharpshooters and at every crossing we ran. When he arrived at the hospital everybody kissed him and cheered him. He had tears in his eyes. I forget his name.

One doctor, a pale man with dark-circled eyes, stood in the courtyard trembling. They shouted "Fascist" to him and said they would send him to trial. Nobody went near him. He made me think of a leper.

The casualties were now coming in fast. The German and Fascist snipers left behind were very good marksmen. They hit everyone in the belly where the chances of surviving were least. If the wound was slight and the partisan had not had any food recently, he sometimes recovered. But if he had had a meal and the bullet had pierced the intestine in more than one place, it was almost always fatal. After the operation, he developed peritonitis and it was the end.

They carried in one boy and laid him on the table. A girl
stood next to him. They were both extremely thin and pale,
very poorly dressed. They looked at each other without
talking, she did not hold his hand.

"Is this your brother?" I asked.

"No, my boy friend," she answered and went on looking
at his suffering face. He died shortly after.

Then a group of boys came in with a wounded companion. They were noisy and excited and armed. One of them
went to the window of the dispensary, where the boy was
lying waiting to be examined. He opened it and started to
shoot.

"Don't shoot from here!" I said.

"Why not? Are you afraid?"

"*You* must be afraid if you come and shoot from a hospital
window risking the lives of the people who come here to be
looked after!"

He got mad, so did I. He stopped shooting.

One child had been shot in the head while he was looking
out of the window. Luckily the bullet had only injured his
skull without cracking the bone.

All the shutters and doors of the streets facing the *viali*
were closed. The people stood in the entrance lobbies not
daring to move.

From time to time I would run home to see how Gianni
was and tell him what was going on. He had a few visitors
to cheer him up. People were now coming out of hiding and
the atmosphere was of great joy mingled with fright and
astonishment at the Allies not arriving.

There were many soldiers who had been wounded during
the war with the Germans and who had been in the hospital
for months. Inevitably, they were being treated with less
care since all the partisan casualties had filled the wards.
The nurses were overwhelmed with work.

One little soldier came to me in the consulting room one afternoon when everybody was resting and asked me if I would change the bandages on his arm. He sat on the cot and turned his head toward the wall. I started to unbandage his wounds and, to my horror, I saw that big white worms were swarming all over his sores. They tumbled to the ground and filled the bandages. I kept myself from screaming, my hands shook. The soldier looked at me with pleading eyes.

I changed his dressing and pretended nothing was wrong. He thanked me and I was ashamed.

Part Five

At last they arrived! The Allies!

The first one I saw was a Scottish officer in a kilt. A sharpshooter shot him as he was walking down the street and they carried him into the hospital. The Italians couldn't believe that men actually did go to war wearing a skirt. They thought it was a tale and they looked at him aghast.

The church bells rang, everyone rushed into the streets. There was a parade to the Palazzo Vecchio—people carrying red flags, shouting, whistling, dancing. They told me to take my veil off, this was freedom. I walked with them, bareheaded in my uniform, until one of the old Red Cross duchesses saw me and told me to go home and put my veil back on. She said this was a bad parade with all those red flags. She had seen this once before after World War I.

I didn't care what she said. I was happy, at last, at last, at last!

I was struck by the Allied jeeps. For some reason I had always figured they would arrive in big American Cadillacs, and, instead, here they were in toylike little open cars. And their smell was completely different from any other army's: soap and strong tea. They streamed in over the bridge they had strung over the Arno and drove all over town. People kissed them, loved them, adored them. They looked pleased, shy, and unconvinced.

As I walked toward the Blue Sisters Clinic I saw a jeep driving slowly in my direction and I looked again and again at the officer in American uniform.

"Puccio!" I shouted.

He stopped. I couldn't believe it. It was Puccio Pucci driving to his palace on the Via Pucci.

"Suni!" he was just as surprised. "What are you doing here?"

"And you?"

I climbed into his jeep and we talked and talked. I told him of Gianni and of Emilio. He told me of the south and the war. I said I wanted to reach Rome as soon as possible but that rumor had it that no passes would be issued for weeks.

"Don't worry," he said. "I'm going back the day after tomorrow. Wear your uniform, and I'll take you with me. Nobody will ask you for a pass."

I ran back to Gianni and told him. I hated to leave him, but from Rome I could get in touch with everyone and find a way of getting him there as soon as possible.

He agreed. His foot was better, but, even with crutches, he could barely get around. But now the Fiat people were back. Friends came to see him.

The nightmare was over.

I sat in the jeep, my blue silk veil blowing in the wind, as excited as a child going for the first time on a voyage. We crossed the Arno on the Allied bridge where the Ponte a Santa Trinita used to be. Along the river Florence was full of rubble but everyone walked around happily. There was color in every corner.

I was madly curious to see this Allied Army that I had waited for with such anxiety. It was like a blind date with a boy whom you are expecting to be fabulous.

I wasn't disappointed. To begin with: there were so many of them and they didn't seem at war at all. It looked like a fantastic parade, a beautiful pageant, a film. They all wore this very light, very clean, cream-colored material. They were shaved, fair, well fed. You felt that they were rich. They were brown, white, black, yellow. They laughed.

We drove down Italy. The countryside was green, the sun was shining. We never even thought about strafing planes.

When we needed gas we just went up to a station and filled the tank. When we were thirsty we stopped and they gave us tea—lovely, strong, dark tea with lots of cream and sugar—or sometimes beer for Puccio. They gave us thick slices of bread as white as snow, covered in butter, and pieces of corned beef that I adored. Everyone was friendly. No one asked you questions. They joked, played, talked. I couldn't get over it. This was war. The other part had been war, too.

The villages we drove by were heaps of rubble. It was difficult to believe anybody could go on living there.

We came to Rome. It was as always lying majestically, saturated with cars, trucks, people, soldiers, officers of a hundred nationalities.

Puccio drove me home. I rang the bell and a British soldier opened the door. He was tall and polite and asked me what was I looking for. I stared at him and he stared at me. He spoke with a very refined cockney accent, eating his words.

"This is my house," I said.

"It has been requisitioned by the Allied Forces," he mumbled, "and is now the residence of Colonel Astley."

At that moment Pasquale, the butler from Turin, Pasqualina, his wife, and their children came running down the stairs.

"Signorina Suni!" they screamed. "Come in, come in. You'll talk to the Colonel when he comes back later. You'll see. They'll find a way. He and the Capitanino, they are nice, they are *signori*."

The poor British soldier was swept aside. What was the

point of talking to someone who obviously wasn't a *signore* and consequently understood nothing.

I hugged Puccio tenderly and walked up the stairs. Pasquale and Pasqualina gave me a report.

As the house was empty, the Allies had requisitioned it. The officers had kept the couple to cook and wait on them and in exchange gave them food for the whole family. The Colonel slept in my mother's room, the Captain in the room which used to be mine—the one I studied in with the red Roman sunsets below me.

I stood, an unexpected visitor, on the terrace of my house, tired and slightly worried.

They arrived late in the afternoon. Colonel Astley was handsome and gray-haired. He was head of the Allied Press Bureau. His ADC was a youngish, very un-English looking Captain, whose name was Patrick Henderson. We looked at one another with suspicion.

"Have a cigarette," the Captain offered me a packet.

"Thank you, I don't smoke."

"Have a drink."

"Thank you, I don't drink."

We stood in embarrassed silence. I wished I did drink and smoke. It would have made things so much easier.

"Where have you come from?" they asked after a while.

"From Switzerland. I crawled under the net and then tried to cross the lines. We had an accident. My brother is still in Florence."

I must have sounded pretty desperate because they very kindly said they would sleep together in my mother's room and I could sleep in the other until we came to some kind of agreement. I said "thank you" very politely and they asked me to join them for dinner. It was served downstairs in the round dining room by Pasquale and the batman, whose name was Smith. There were candles on the table and the food was good: Allied rations plus Pasqualina's skill and Pasquale's supervising.

Pasqualina told me that Smith had asked her how old I was and when she had answered twenty-two, he said the Captain had thought I was thirty and said I acted like forty. I smiled and went to my bedroom to think things over, but I was so tired I fell asleep.

I woke up in the Roman end-of-summer heat and could not remember where I was.

I still had nothing to wear except the skirt and the two shirts my cousin had given me when I had spent the night with her, but I did have a bicycle and the unlimited use of a telephone. The Allies had realized after a few days in Rome that almost every citizen in town spent half of his time on the telephone. They issued an order that whoever put in a call and was on the phone for more than three minutes would be cut off. It changed the Roman way of life. They had to find something to do during those hours they were accustomed to spending so pleasantly.

Through Fiat and the diplomatic corps I sent my mother a message that Gianni and I were safe. It was the first news she got from us since we had left Switzerland.

I went to the hospital and saw the nurses from the school who were my friends. They told me the wards were full of casualties from motor-car accidents, run-over people, children. There were no medicines, no bandages, everything had to be bought very expensively on the black market. The patients were very badly cared for.

I went home. I wasn't in the mood for sadness yet.

Puccio had told me while we were driving down that my Navy hero had been released from the Spanish prison and was now working with the Allies. I looked forward to seeing him. It was nice to know one had a friend to rely on who was sensible and brave. I had written him a letter when he was in prison saying that I had always thought that he would do the right thing and that I understood him even if others criticized him.

I sat alone in my room and used my privileged Allied phone to ring him up and have a talk with him. He answered the telephone.

"Hello," I said, rather nervous, "it's Suni."

"How are you?" He was evidently surprised and his voice was cold. "How is your mother? How are your brothers and sisters? What have you been doing?"

I tried to answer but he said, "Good-by. I can't stay on the telephone for more than three minutes or they will cut my line."

"Don't worry," I assured him, "I have Allied officers in the house. I can stay on the telephone as long as I like."

"But I cannot. I'll call you next week." And he hung up.

I rested my head on the back of the armchair and sobbed desperately for a long time. I felt alone, abandoned, motherless, unwanted. I loathed the world, men, my Navy hero that I had cherished in my heart as being brave and understanding when he was only selfish and proud. I cried and cried, then took a bath and went to dinner with my British hosts.

"What did you do today?" they asked, making polite conversation.

"Mostly I have been crying."

"Why crying?"

I told them and they laughed. They asked my Navy hero's name. They knew of him and said, "You can't be crying about that pompous Victoria Cross. He must be a fool to behave like that."

I agreed, we talked, we drank some wine, I started to laugh. I imitated Smith speaking his very refined cockney on discovering me at the door. They told me how terrible they thought I was when they saw me standing on the terrace in my nurse's uniform. They told me about their work; I told them about my life.

After that they would bring people for lunch and dinner. Commanding Generals, actresses who came over to entertain the troops, men from the British Secret Service or the OSS, officers back from the front or just in from the States. I sat at the head of the table and they joked about my leaving the room the instant the meal was finished. I learned to sit on while they drank coffee and smoked.

We forgot to make arrangements about what we would do with the house. It was a blissful combination.

Of course I fell in love with the "Capitanino," as Pasqualina called him.

He had an Italian girl friend, an actress, just for a change. In the evenings he would go and visit her but when he came home, I would call to him and he would come and talk, sitting at my bedside with a glass of whisky in his hand. He told me of how he handed out his press releases to the waiting reporters and how they whizzed off to their telephones while he stood alone and empty-handed in the middle of the room with his morning's work gone.

He imitated everybody's accent or way of speaking and, as it was a habit we both had, we would go on for hours taking off on the silly people we had met during the day. I also imitated his girl friend who, being Italian and not speaking English, had turned her name into a French-sounding nickname that she must have thought more exotic. But there he laughed less.

The Colonel went on leave and Patrick stayed on. We changed rooms; I stayed in my mother's and he in the one that was mine.

*M*y friends would come for meals, too. Topazia and Galvano and, of course, Raimondo, but he hated the idea of having to be punctual and my Allies hated the idea that he would be late, so it wasn't a great success. He would come and visit me at night instead, as was his custom. He lay at the foot of my bed and cried because this girl made his life hell and would end up by destroying him. He had come back from the south with a radio transmitter and had communicated with the Allies from a secret hiding place. Now he was a civilian again.

"You can't be so banal as to have a crush on the British officer who lives in your house." Raimondo was furious. "It's what every woman in Rome is doing and it's not like you."

It certainly was very banal but it is true that obvious things are born for obvious reasons. An Allied officer in August 1944 in Rome carried with him the aura of freedom and peace. How could you not fall in love with freedom and peace?

Patrick laughed.

"Nonsense," he exclaimed when I told him I was in love with him. "I am old, almost thirty-four; I am British. You will die of shame in a few years time when you remember you said you were in love with me."

I waited for him to come home. I would say to myself, "If now he has reached the garage and put his car in, he will be walking up the road and will arrive at the door in five and a half minutes," then begin again: "If now he has . . ." until I heard the noise of the door shutting echoing up the hall and his footsteps came up the stairs and I called "Patrick?" and he opened the door and said, "You are not still awake, you silly girl? I'll brush my teeth and come and say good-night to you."

He would come back and sit with me and I was crazy with joy. We laughed and joked. I was mad about his British humor, the smooth skin on his hairless chest that I saw through his shirt when he unbuttoned it to take his tie off, his sweet brotherly attitude.

Once he put both his hands on my shoulders and kissed me. Then he said, "Forgive me," and went away.

I hadn't forgotten about Gianni but it wasn't easy to get him from Florence to Rome. The Allies had forbidden the movement of civilians and released very few passes for people not traveling in military vehicles. Gianni was in no condition to travel in a jeep.

Then one day I met Dino Philipson, a politician who had been south with the Badoglio government. He had lived for years, practically interned as an anti-Fascist, in his villa between Florence and the sea. He was looking for someone to take him to Florence and said that if I could produce a chauffeur-driven car, he would bring Gianni back with him. At Fiat's they were delighted with the solution, and off he went.

Now, with Gianni arriving, the arrangement with the Allies became very difficult. We shifted rooms and beds once more, but then the Colonel and the Captain found an apartment that they could rent and left the house. I was sorry to see both of them go. With the Colonel I had a marvelous understanding and loved to know he would be there when I got home. With Patrick I was in love, but I knew it wouldn't have worked with Gianni in the house. They would have misunderstood each other and there would have been the kind of strain I cannot stand.

So Gianni arrived, on crutches, very thin, very pale, with an abscess forming in the middle of his forehead, his hair cut short, and a look of uncertainty. All the girls who came to see him fell in love with him. His being crippled excited their romantic penchant.

I studied medicine at the University of Rome. I was delighted when a fellow student told me I was the only person in the amphitheater where we had classes who looked like a doctor.

I went to the hospital often, not as a nurse, but to see what was going on. It was true that conditions were disastrous. One little Neapolitan boy lay in his bed with a shaved head and big pleading eyes. Both his legs were broken at the thigh bone and no one did anything about it because they had no plaster bandages with which to make a cast.

The boy was alone; he had been run over in Naples and the Allies had carried him to Rome. An incredible number of abandoned children crowded Italy. They were lost or orphaned or had followed some soldier who picked them up or had simply walked away for adventure's sake.

This little boy never grumbled. He would hold my hand and ask me for *pasta* with tomato sauce. Pasqualina would cook him a bowl of macaroni with a lot of Parmesan cheese and tomato sauce and I would carry it to him.

"*Signuri!*" he called to me, smiling, when I walked into the ward, pulling his head up from the pillow.

When he saw the bowl his eyes lit up with happiness. He would put it on his chest and eat up to the last drop of sauce.

Then he developed osteomyelitis in his fractured legs. He got worse and worse, his dark skin like a rubber diving suit that got tighter every day. When he didn't eat his *pasta* I knew it was the end. He clutched at me, feverish, his eyes imploring, for what, I never knew. He died without ever mentioning his father or mother or any other name.

The day after that, a little girl with blond curls falling down to her shoulders was brought in, her legs broken. She was alone. I got one of my friends to come to the hospital and pretend she was the child's aunt and sign the papers to take her out of the ward. I asked Patrick to come with his car and transport her to the University Clinic, where I knew they would look after her properly.

He came, carried the child, then took me home and said, "Suni, you can't fight the world. What is the good? After this child there will be ten others, hundreds in all the hospitals of Italy. Are you going to steal the children out of this ward every day?"

I had no answer.

I wanted to get some ambulances that would follow the Allied Army and carry the civilian casualties to hospital. The Army ambulances were not allowed to transport them and I knew what had happened when Gianni was lying on the floor with his foot shattered.

I managed to get five Fiat cars that would be turned into ambulances. I managed to get the Red Cross to authorize the formation of a new corps with girl drivers enrolled as Red Cross volunteers. I managed to get the Allies to issue free gas and K-rations when we would follow the Army. I managed to get ten girls who would volunteer for a training period and then to enlist until the war ended.

The greatest difficulty was the tires, but I went to Allied

Headquarters, and I think it was General Mark Clark himself who gave orders that we should be given tires for our ambulances.

*G*ianni was much better. He used a cane but hopped around quite gaily. He was going north as a liaison officer with one of the Italian regiments fighting with the Allies and would soon be back in uniform.

My ambulances were almost ready but something was always going wrong. At Red Cross Headquarters they obliged us to name as *capo gruppo* a nurse whose only merit was that her brother had been shot as a partisan. They were afraid that otherwise the group would be criticized as reactionary. (The girls were, in fact, mostly friends of mine and from aristocratic families: Topazia, Marilise Carafa, Letizia Boncompagni; my name was even worse.) We had to accept their choice or we would not get authorization to leave.

Suddenly I began to go out with boys. They took me dancing; they ran after me; they kissed me—I enjoyed it. Now when I told Patrick I was in love with him, it was only a half-truth. Ottavio Montezemolo, whom the Allies had freed from a prisoners' camp because of his exceptional war record, visited me often. His full name, in very Piedmontese fashion, was Lanza Cordero di Montezemolo.

When Raimondo heard that I was going out with him, he brought me, as a present, a silver plaque with Saint Christopher engraved on it along with the words, "LOOK AT ME AND NOT AT LANZA." I put it on the dashboard of my ambulance. Raimondo said, as always, that he loved me and that when the war ended we would get married. He traveled from Rome to Sicily to satisfy his nervousness, still fascinating me and driving me insane.

My Navy hero asked me to give him, the red cross I wore around my neck, when I went away. I did.

But I liked Dario best of all. He was a good-looking Milanese boy who wore horn-rimmed spectacles. He was Jewish and a liaison officer with the Eighth Army; he was in love with me, and we had a good time together.

Topazia said I was promiscuous.

I said, "You can't be faithful unless you are in love."

We stood in a row. Gray-blue battle-dress jackets and skirts, with a matching cap that Topazia loathed; our five ambulances behind us. The military bishop gave us his blessing and we drove north. Soon the war ended.

Now that Italy had been completely liberated, the partisans were controlling all the towns north of Florence.

Mussolini, with his mistress and a few followers, had been shot and strung up by the heels in Piazzale Loreto. The crowds walked in front of the show shooting bullets into the bodies.

Our group was divided. Two ambulances were posted in Bologna: Topazia and Annamaria, Marilise and myself. We slept very little, at unlikely hours at the nursing school of the hospital. The Allies gave us K-rations, those mysterious brown boxes that were, for us Italians, an unending surprise; the meat, the biscuit, the chocolate, the cigarette. We ate them while we drove down the roads that looked like Swiss cheese. On some of them that had been shelled and bombed more heavily, you could only proceed at a crawl. When we were sent on some out-of-the-way road to carry a child to a sanatorium or a nun to an old-age rest home, the driving seemed bliss.

A group of people was forever waiting for us in the courtyard of the hospital to beg us to pick up some wounded or sick person and carry him to the hospital. They quarreled as to who would be the first. They tried to bribe us. They brought us presents; a loaf of white bread or two eggs, or a medal of the Madonna. Mothers in despairing immobility came to life to run after the ambulances saying, "Please."

I drove and drank coffee; washed my face and drove off again. When I slept I dreamed of people downstairs saying "Please," and waiting. I remembered the German soldiers who were too tired to drive Gianni to the hospital. I got up again, drank more coffee, and drove off once more.

I forgot I was tired and lived in a sort of drunken elation, as if my body belonged to somebody else.

Some doctors were helpful. Others hated us because the Allies gave us free gas and we were independent. They behaved as if we were necessarily whores for the Allies.

I told one doctor that the Allies had a drug called "penicillin" which killed an infection in an incredibly short time. He howled with laughter.

"You believe these tales? My God, you must be silly."

There was no point in arguing. I just drove on.

We took some little girls home from a sanatorium on a hill near Modena. They told us of how the nuns would punish them by keeping them on their knees in front of an open window during the winter, or by making them stand all night next to the bed where one of their roommates was dying.

One of the children had an old woman's face with papery pale skin. She told us coldly that, anyway, she would be dead before next winter. Even her hair was smelly and gray with sickness.

We drove over mined roads into a destroyed village, where the sweetish smell of rotting corpses was as strong as decaying flowers in an airless room, to pick up a boy who had been lying for weeks with his legs broken.

We rushed a baby dying of enteritis from the long, calm Po embankments to the nearest hospital, the young mother clutching to her breast the livid, panting child.

We drove people home to die and picked up casualties from motor-car accidents left lying on the roads.

We also drove to Ravenna and the Adriatic, and sat for a few moments looking at the sea, empty, green-blue, and melancholic.

We fell asleep in the midst of endless discussions. Topazia and I had a different outlook on life. She said that as long as there was something good, it did not matter if other things were wrong. I said that as long as there were bad people and wrong things, the good would always be trampled upon. We woke up and went on discussing as we put our clothes on.

With Marilise in the ambulance we talked about other things; mostly about boys. She irritated and amused me. She was so different from me. Her pretty mouth, with a red, red lipstick, her floating hair and futile remarks, her way of taking life as it came, never thinking that anything inside yourself could change whatever was going to happen to you. I thought that people could change the world.

Someone told Topazia that my mother was in Milan. She had walked over the border into Italy. I was dying of impatience to see her, and as soon as a possible excuse arose we drove off at night to carry a patient to Milan.

At every crossroad groups of people stood asking for a lift. It was the only available means of transportation. There were many partisans in shorts with arm bands and a red handkerchief around their neck. We would pick up whoever could be fitted into the ambulance. One partisan armed with a machine gun and a revolver crowded in front with Marilise and myself.

He was arrogant and odious. He told us he had been to Sicily to buy nylon stockings that he would sell on the black market when he got up north.

"I want to go to Turin," he said, "and if you don't take me where I want to go I will point my gun at you and you jolly well will."

I didn't answer.

"Anyway," he went on, "we are the bosses now. At last, even Agnelli has been executed. The radio said so this morning, and high time it was."

I still said nothing. When we came to the next MP post I slowed down and stopped in front of the two black, smiling American soldiers, and said slowly and loudly in English, "Please get this man off my ambulance."

They opened the door and lifted him out. He was so surprised he didn't say a word. I drove off not knowing if what he had said was true.

I was so tired I had hallucinations. I saw people hanging from trees, and then realized they were only branches. I saw water where there was none and lights in the sky. We drove to the apartment where my mother was staying and found Gianni had arrived there, too. Between me and my mother there was that same embarrassment as if we came from two different worlds, a loving incomprehension.

My grandfather was alive. The partisans had occupied his house, except for two rooms left to his wife and himself, but he was forbidden to enter the Fiat plant. He would walk there, look up at the windows, shake his head, and say, "I built it, all of it."

My mother was depressed. The people who had boasted they wouldn't say hello to her would then stand up and kiss her hand when she walked up to them in public. Life had gone from the dramatic to the theatrical.

The telephone rang. "Who is it?" I asked.

"Urbano Rattazzi."

"You must be mad. Aren't they looking for you?"

"May I come and see you?"

"Isn't it dangerous for you to walk in the streets?"

"I'll come on a bicycle."

I put down the receiver and said, "Do you think they will kill him?"

I lunched at Berta's in the apartment of her husband's family. At the head of the table sat a woman in her sixties carrying, with great dignity, a round, gray head completely shaved by the partisans. Most of the women and girls who had been shaved wore a scarf around their heads and it was unusual to meet such deliberate, brave indifference as this aunt of Berta's showed. It was also difficult to make conversation.

I went back to where my mother was staying and Urbano arrived. He asked me if I could drive Valerio Borghese to Florence in my ambulance. As Commander-in-Chief of the Decima Mas, a Fascist regiment that had been fighting the partisans, he was condemned to death and they were searching for him all over.

I gulped and considered the situation for a moment

before I said yes. Thank God, someone else took him in another ambulance.

Urbano told me that after the Nettuno front had collapsed and the Decima had been transferred north to fight the partisans, he had resigned as ADC to Valerio Borghese and retired to his villa in Sestri Levante. He would not fight against Italians. Now he was trying to save his commander's life.

He, too, had been threatened. He asked if he could go and stay in Forte dei Marmi, where nobody knew who he was, so he would be out of the way for a while.

The house had neither been bombed nor robbed. The caretakers had hidden and saved everything, and as it was one of the few houses left with beds and sheets, everyone we knew who was driving from Rome to Turin would go there to sleep. Every hotel was requisitioned by the Allies and unless you had friends in whose houses you could stay, it was difficult to move around.

My mother said Urbano could go to Forte dei Marmi and I went back to Bologna promising I would visit him as soon as I could get away on rest leave.

I was driving through a small town one afternoon and remembered this was the town where Baldetti lived, the boy I had said good-by to at the station of Rome the day Badoglio had announced the surrender of Italy. I was curious to know what had happened to the blue-eyed, blue-uniformed, blue-ribboned pilot with his blond hair combed back from his forehead over his shy impudent smile. He had written me a few letters when he had got home but they were Italian letters, full of sentimentality and very little news.

I knew his address and we found the house. An old woman came to the door and opened it very slightly. She held it with both hands and looked suspiciously at our uniforms and ambulance.

"Is Sergeant Baldetti here?" I asked.

"No," she answered quickly. "No, he is not here."

"Where is he? Is he all right?"

"I don't know," she answered curtly, and was about to close the door.

"Are you his mother?" I insisted. "I would like to leave a message. My name is Suni Agnelli. Tell him I came to say hello."

"You are Signorina Agnelli?" She opened the door. "It is you who looked after him in the hospital? Come in, come in. I am sorry, I didn't know it was you."

We entered. It was a country farmhouse with a courtyard and a barn. We sat on two wooden chairs, she wrung her hands, tears came to her eyes.

"Is your son alive?" I couldn't make out what had happened. "Is something the matter?"

She looked at me and then at Marilise. We must have seemed pretty harmless.

"Wait a moment," she said, leaving, and disappearing into the barn. Marilise opened her eyes wide and made a typical Neapolitan gesture that meant, "We'll see."

The woman opened the door from the barn into the courtyard, looked right, then left, then beckoned behind her.

A boy followed. He had hay in his hair, a striped brown and beige shirt, and the look that only fugitives have. A hunted man or a hunted animal become similar; sensitive, pathetic, as if they were already in the clutch of that death which they are trying to escape.

I stood up and walked toward him. We shook hands. He said thank you for coming. I could feel he was ashamed at being found in this condition, hiding in his own house. He ran his fingers through his greasy hair and brushed the dust off his shirt sleeves.

I didn't like to ask questions. He offered little information. I talked about my ambulance and my work. The mother said times were terrible; we all agreed. I said we had a lot to do and would have to be moving on; I would come back and see him another time. We all knew it wasn't true and said good-by with false gaiety.

I drove my ambulance in silence; even Marilise could not cheer me up.

Behind the walls of the houses, behind the doors on the straight, half-empty street, I imagined people afraid of walking out into the sun.

*O*ur *capo gruppo* was stationed somewhere in the north and she would unexpectedly appear in Bologna, to control our work, and then drive south. I was told that she filled the tank of her ambulance, sold the gas on the black market, then filled it again at the next Allied gas pump. I made inquiries and discovered it was true.

Then I got proof that she used the ambulance to go to the south of Italy and buy merchandise which she would sell on the black market in the northern towns.

It was too easy. No one would control her ambulance. They gave her free gas wherever she went, and she had precedence on every road. I despised this woman for profiteering and loathed her for doing this with something I had put into her hands.

I went to Rome and asked for an appointment with the President of the Red Cross. He was a very nice Left-minded archeologist.

I told him what was going on. He shrugged his shoulders. I explained that the Allies had implicitly trusted us, that I, personally, when I had obtained our gas cards, had made myself responsible for how they would be used. Couldn't he see this was a breach of trust? He could not allow this. It was the name of the Italian Red Cross that was at stake.

He sighed, "Go on with your work. We can't send her away, it would create a scandal and make us unpopular."

"But, she is a thief!" I cried. "She is using an ambulance that could be saving a person's life to make money for herself. Don't you see how dishonest it is?"

"Pretend you don't know. It's the best thing you can do."

I walked out of his office without saying good-by. I drove back to Bologna choking with fury and tears and talked to Topazia all night long.

Even she did not understand. I explained that we—I, she, Marilise, and all the others—were conniving with this woman. We became implicitly responsible for what she did. Having given our word to the Allies meant nothing if we let her tell lies. When she stole, we were stealing with her.

They said I exaggerated. If there was nothing we could do about it we had better not think about it.

I thought I would go mad. I drove that ambulance of mine day and night, trying to forget.

Ottavio Montezemolo sent word that he was stationed with his regiment somewhere not far away. We drove past it one day, and I went into the regiment's precinct. A jeep, with a colonel and his staff, was coming toward us. They told us where we would find Captain Montezemolo. We stood talking to him while leaning against the ambulance under the trees of an alley.

Suddenly we saw the jeep driving back toward us. The colonel was as red as a pepper and gesticulating. He got off the jeep and walked toward me.

"I did not know who you were," he shouted at me, "otherwise I never would have allowed you into my regiment's precinct. Nobody whose name is Agnelli will be received where I am in command."

"I happen to be very proud of the name Agnelli," I answered.

"Your pride is wrong." He grew redder and sweat poured down his face. "It is not the pride of an Italian!"

Ottavio Montezemolo stood at attention.

"*Signor Colonello,*" he said quietly, "it is I who invited the Signorina to come here."

"You were wrong to do so!" he screamed, by now totally out of control. "And get her out of here!"

"*Signor Colonello,*" he answered, "I ask you to accept my resignation as an officer in your regiment."

The colonel got back into his jeep and waved the driver off.

I drove my ambulance back onto the public road and stopped.

"That colonel ought to be kicked in the balls!" Marilise said.

Ottavio arrived with his car. Another officer followed him to ask me to tell Captain Montezemolo to withdraw his resignation as he was an honor to the regiment. I laughed and laughed with tears running down my cheeks.

"Withdraw your resignation, Ottavio," I said. "What good would it do?"

Ottavio came to see me at our hospital that evening. We sat on the grass and I thanked him for being the way he was.

It was August. I lost the chain I carried around my neck with Raimondo's ring hanging from it, I lost my papers, I lost everything. I asked for a rest leave and went to Forte dei Marmi.

Part Six

Dario met me in Forte dei Marmi. We went swimming. I washed my hair with water in which they had cooked cinders. We walked on the empty beach and sat on the ground under the pine trees. The house was full of friends. Everyone slept with everyone else without any discretion. With the end of the war had come an explosion of sex.

We ate mussels, fish, black bread. The "Capannina" was open and people danced all night, barefoot. The Allies brought DDT and whisky. Black soldiers drove up and down in jeeps from a village of folly in the *pineta* of Migliarino, where girls, children and soldiers lived in a crazy orgy, stealing everything they could get their hands on from the enormous Allied deposits near Livorno.

The black market was rampant. You could buy any American goods: guns, uniforms, food, beauty products, liquor, medicines.

Urbano was studying for his law-school examination. He was thin, very thin, pale, and his green eyes shone. I walked past him going to the seaside with Dario holding my arm. Urbano looked up at me from his book.

"Your eyes are as green as fresh almonds," I said, and walked on thinking of the furry touch of the almond hull when you pick it off the tree.

Dario went back to Rome, where his Allied boss was expecting him, and promised he would be back soon.

My mother went back to Switzerland.

In the empty house Urbano and I were alone; we suffered from the same shattered illusions. I sat talking to him under the pine trees. I looked into his eyes and smiled. When we kissed, I called him *"mandorlino."*

Dario returned three days later, early in the morning. He dashed into my room, Urbano was sitting on my bed.

"Come to the sea," he said, "let's go and swim."

"Sit down, Dario," I said. "I want to tell you something. Urbano and I are going to get married."

He laughed.

"What a pretty joke," he said.

"It's not a joke."

"All right," he added, "you are going to get married. Go ahead. But, now, stop fooling around and come and swim with me. I'm hot."

He stopped at the door, turned around and looked at us.

"You're crazy!" he cried. "You are raving mad!" and he ran down the stairs and drove off in his car.

I went with Urbano to meet his mother. She was worried that I might ask for a cocktail. When she saw me without any make-up, she couldn't believe her eyes.

Then we went to my grandfather's in Turin. He took Urbano to the window, looked into his face, and said, "He'll be all right."

Nine days after I had left Bologna, Topazia, Marilise, and Annamaria came for the wedding. I wore an old dress and a new pair of wooden *zoccoli*, a blue cardigan, a pink ribbon on my bra, and a borrowed piece of lace on my head.

Topazia drove me to the church of Forte dei Marmi in her ambulance. Gianni walked me to the altar limping slightly. When he left me standing there he smiled and squeezed my fingers.

Urbano was waiting.

I looked into his green eyes and thought that life would be a green lawn, green as his eyes, full of running children.

February 28, 1974
New York